Hawai'i in War and Peace

A MEMOIR
Second Edition.

by
Bill Fernandez

www.kauaibillfernandez.com facebook: Bill Fernandez Hawaiian Author

Dedication page photograph: Bill on steps of United States Supreme Court, 1948

ISBN: 1539800423
ISBN 13: 9781539800422
Lirbrary of Congress Control Number: 2016918277
CreateSpace Independent Publishing Platform
North Charleston, South Carolina

Contents

Dedication

I dedicate this book to
my parents,
Willliam Antonne and
Agnes Scharsch
Fernandez.

Acknowledgments

The Hawaiian ethic of *ohana* (family) means no one accomplishes alone. We are who we are today because of those who came before us and who are with us along our path of life. I particularly say *mahalo* (thank you) to my teachers, especially those at Kamehameha Schools who turned a barefoot boy into a serious student. Vernon Trimble, my sophomore class advisor, stands out in my memories as a strong influence urging me to attend college.

Thanks go to my editor and friend, Bill Bernhardt, who taught me about commas and tries to mold me into a good writer.

There are many others who helped along the way, encouraging me to continue writing. Thanks to the Kaua'i Historical Society for honoring me by including my books in their publication sales. Bill Buley of the Garden Island Newspaper and his wife Marianne encourage me in many ways.

Without the support, wisdom, and encouragement of my loving wife, Judith, I could not have written the three books I have published. All the credit for what I have written goes to her.

Introduction

Many people have asked me to write a second memoir after reading about my first fourteen years of life growing up on a tiny dot in the Pacific, Kaua'i, in the Hawaiian Islands. "How did you manage to end up going to Stanford University and then become a judge in Santa Clara County?"

Kaua'i Kids in Peace and War described my barefoot years exploring the ocean, challenging sugar cane trains, and making tin canoes. The outside world intruded in a dramatic way when Pearl Harbor was bombed by the Japanese in 1941. In a few months thousands of soldiers from the U.S. mainland descended on our dot in the Pacific Ocean. They brought with them knowledge of a great world that existed beyond our island. They brought with them wealth which propelled small businesses, like my father's struggling movie theater, into prosperity.

My prior book ended in 1944, as, at age fourteen, I boarded an airplane to go to Kamehameha Schools for children of Hawaiian ancestry in Honolulu. In my time for many of native blood this was their only opportunity to receive a worthwhile education.

Hawai'i in War and Peace begins after that plane lands on an urbanized island and I confront a puzzling world of a strict military school, forced to wear a uniform, stiff shoes, and keep my room clean for inspection. The United States military presence had created a different world from Kaua'i. Discrimination and racism were evident between the mostly Caucasian GIs and locals, primarily Asian and Native Hawaiians.

As a barefoot boy I had low aspirations. There were not many opportunities for a Hawaiian kid beyond being a fisherman or pineapple picker. This was not what my parents had in mind for me. Would I have the wisdom to take the stepping stone that a Kamehameha education provided and seek to achieve a socially useful life?

Hele Mai – join me in my adventures as I struggle into adulthood.
Aloha nui loa,
Bill Fernandez

www.kauaibillfernandez.com
facebook: Bill Fernandez Hawaiian Author

Other titles by author:

Non-Fiction
Rainbows Over Kapaa
Kaua'i Kids in Peace and War

Fiction

Cult of Ku, a Hawaiian Murder Mystery
John Tana, An Adventure Tale of Old Hawai'i

A *Akahai*
Kindness, expressed with tenderness.

L *Lōkahi*
Unity, expressed with harmony.

O *'Olu'olu*
Agreeable, expressed with pleasantness.

H *Ha'aha'a*
Humility, expressed with modesty.

A *Ahonui*
Patience, expressed with perseverance.

Aloha: It's Kaua'i's Spirit

CHAPTER 1

Kamehameha Schools

Without warning the animal attacked me. Teeth ripped cloth and bit into flesh, blood flowed staining my only pants. Man's best friend succeeded in destroying any chance I had of creating a favorable impression when I arrived at Kamehameha. Add to this disaster, it is Monday night and boarding school has been in session for a week.

Why am I late? Answer, I had not been chosen from among the slots available for children from Kaua'i. A new eighth grader from my island had started on time, but got homesick and dropped out. Not a laughing matter. Oh no. It is tough to leave your home where life is simple and understandable. If you obey the plantation rules, you'll be okay. It's different in the big city and in a boarding school. There are new rules, but most important, you must learn to fend for yourself when the trouble starts and it does.

Why did I come? Kamehameha Schools' offer to accept me solved my parents' problem. My dad had retired to California and Mom wanted to join him, but I was an anchor holding her back. With acceptance, I could be shipped to Honolulu where I would be educated, fed, and boarded all for $60 a year. What a deal.

At the city airport Aunt Emily picked me up and drove me to her home. She said Uncle Arthur would take me up the mountain to Kamehameha. But they are not my aunt and uncle. Arthur's brother had been married to my real aunt. But he abandoned her and four cousins in Georgia. Our Kaua'i family had paid their way, during wartime, to return the family to Hawai'i.

Why tell you this? I had no blood relatives in Honolulu to meet me and instead had to depend on a stranger to gather me up and take me to school.

While I had waited in the back yard for Arthur to return from work the family cur snarled. You know the g-r-r sound dog's make when they don't like you. Why he was angry I don't know. I hadn't given him trouble. I tried to pet the little beast, but he cocked his head, stared at me, and trotted away. It is when I turned my back that the wily animal struck.

I pushed my small brown suitcase into him to free my pants from his teeth. The critter let go. I spied a wooden chair nearby and I leaped on it. I was trapped. But, I stood high enough that he couldn't reach me, though he tried. My case made a good shield to fend off his leaps to bite my leg. I didn't call for help, it seemed cowardly. Nor did I bash the dog, not a good way to make friends with a new family. I stood on my perch and defended myself from the aggressive animal.

The cur got tired and slunk away. I thought to make it into the house. I stepped down and he streaked out of its hiding place heading for my legs. Dogs know to do that. It's the fastest way to bring a giant down and then they can tear you apart.

But I had a plan to meet such a sneaky attack, the matador ploy. You've seen the movies of the brave bullfighter facing the horned black bull with his sword outstretched. I seized the chair and turned its four legs into the beast. Its charge faltered. It skipped right. I met the maneuver with a thrust of the chair. Each move the animal made I countered. Unable to bite me the dog yielded the field of battle. I strode to a gated fence and let myself out of the back yard.

Taking my scuffed shoes off, I entered the home and asked for needle and thread. I didn't know what to do with them since cleaning, sewing, and cooking my mom did. Emily saw the tear in the pants leg and mended it, while I cleaned my injuries in the bathroom.

Dusk set in, Arthur arrived. I grabbed my suitcase and got into his car. In silence we motored up a winding mountain road heading toward a group of stone buildings. As we got closer I thought I would see Doctor Frankenstein preparing to garner lightning from the sky to give life to his creature. Macabre thoughts caused by my first glimpse of this new school, but movies make impressions and what I observed was not like any school that existed on Kaua'i.

Arthur brought the car to a halt in a parking area by a large administrative building. Adjacent was a green field, protected on two sides by a black rock wall. At the far end stood a lighted building from which sounds of robust activity came.

We left the car and headed towards an open-air counter where we met a red-faced man, his head crowned by a marvelous shock of white hair. We identified ourselves. The man said, "Bill Caldwell." I was handed over and Arthur left. I suspected he was relieved to be rid of an unwanted legacy.

Caldwell took me to a supply room and began pulling out clothes and shoes. From a rack he took a grey-blue uniform. "Looks about your size," he said. The coat fit, but the coarse wool abraded my skin. I realized how Christian monks must have suffered in their hair shirts. The warmth of the room made me sweat. Whooping and hollering erupted outside as a passel of young boys in tan uniforms wearing light brown ties roared past.

"You're hungry?" Caldwell said.

I nodded and he hustled me to the lighted building where young boys were busing dishes. "I'll get you something to eat and then you head over to Kamehameha dormitory, report to Mills."

After gobbling food, I rushed out the door with my stack of new clothes and shoes, but became immediately bewildered. There were so many buildings and stairs. I saw a student and asked him, "Where is Kam dorm?"

"Eh brah, this is not a Chinese school. You want Kamehameha dormitory and it's up the stairs and to the right."

Kamehameha Schools at the top of a steep hill meant there
were many stairs to climb. This was my dorm.

Not a good start, I thought as I began to climb. There were a hundred steps to the landing that led to my assigned dormitory. I found Mills and he gave me a third floor room number and said, "Lights out at 8:30. No noise after or else. Don't leave your room until the morning bugle sounds. Breakfast is at 6:30 then report to the farmer at lower field for work. Classes start at 8:30 sharp. Dismissed."

I raced toward the third floor, but halted when Mills shouted, "Hey kid! You're supposed to say, 'yes sir' and salute. Come back here."

I fretted because it was thirty minutes to lights out. But his order rang clear. I walked back, placed my clothes and brown suitcase on the floor, stood and saluted as I had seen it done in the movies.

"Sloppy. Stand at attention. Place your left hand at the side by the seam of your trousers. Shoes at a forty-five degree angle. Elbow out to the side, fingers of the right hand pressed together, right arm bent. Hold your position until I salute back. Oh, you are really a hick. Stick your chin out, stand straight, keep your eyes on me. You get demerits if you're not a good soldier and too many demerits means after hours work and confinement to school."

Mills saluted and waved me away, a look of disgust on his face. I hiked upstairs wondering if I could transform from a country kid to a real soldier. I had no choice but to do so. Mom had rented out the family home and I didn't have a place to go.

I found my room. Met my roommate, also from Kaua'i, bathed, and went to bed. The dormitory, like all the buildings on Kapalama Heights, is made of concrete. It is plain, cold, and drafty. I shivered as I pulled the military olive brown blanket over me, dreading the new life that would unfold in the days ahead.

Class of 1949 at Kamehameha Schools.
I am in the front row third from right

CHAPTER 2

Pearl Harbor

A strident noise summoned me. I clutched the army blanket hoping to hold onto the dream of home on Kaua'i. But in an instant, the disturbing sound was replaced by the gong of a bell forcing me to wake up. Outside my room noise erupted.

My roommate slid from the upper bunk, rocking the bed so hard I feared it would turn over. "Eh, get up," he said. "Work detail."

"What?" I said.

"Got to head to lower field and start raking."

"Eat first?"

"No, after."

We hustled into our clothes and I followed him. He ran down stairs, out the door, and headed onto the long descending stairway leading to our work place. Negotiating the steps two at a time was not as bad as the long run over a green field and then a sprint downward on a wide macadamized road.

Dawn pinked the sky as the unseen sun began its rise. I would soon learn that this is not correct. Although the Catholic Church once preached that the sun revolved around the earth, the truth is the other way around. This is the reason you get educated, to learn the facts. But the illusion that the earth is the center of the universe is hard to dispel. Just like finding out that we only see half of the moon and it has no intrinsic light. Its shine in the night is a reflection of the sun's rays.

Kamehameha Schools is built on top of a mountain. Why, I do not know, for it is difficult to get to as well as hard to run away from. Maybe that is the reason for being high up, it's like a penitentiary for wayward boys. But the views are magnificent. I paused to drink in the beauty unfolding as the darkness flew from the light. Pearl Harbor lay several miles below me, smoke rising from facilities next to its lakes.

It is amazing that I would be allowed to see it, for I had heard many stories of the secrecy surrounding the great naval base. I guess, since it is September of 1944, with the Nazis being beaten in Europe and McArthur rooting out the Japanese in the Philippines, we didn't have to worry about spies.

The view of Honolulu and the airport, at the edge of Pearl Harbor, from Kamehameha Schools.

I fantasized, reliving that fatal day. I saw the first wave of airplanes speeding down the slot toward Pearl Harbor. Other aircraft had come around the Wai'anae range, the sun beaming upon them and the eight battleships lying at anchor. They dropped their bombs. The radio announcer screamed, "We are under attack. This is no drill."

The Japanese bombing of Pearl Harbor in 1941
struck the ammunition magazine of the destroyer Shaw.

What had been unreal, unbelievable, three years before lay in front of me. What had existed only in censored news reports and rumors was real. "Seeing is believing," Ripley said.

Before the Japanese struck, the plantations did what they wanted to. This absolutism changed with war. The military exercised its authority and the plantations obeyed. The monolith of power that controlled us developed cracks.

Japan planned to dominate the Pacific. They couldn't win. But their efforts helped island people break out of the plantation cocoon that imprisoned us. From on top of the hill, I saw the world in a new light. It's like I lived in a grass shack without openings, and suddenly I am transported to a house with many windows.

I lost sight of my roommate, and this awakened me from my daydreaming. I speeded up. Despite being asthmatic diving had toughened me.

The road ended in steps whittled into a red dirt slope and I saw a teacher and other boys in a rock-strewn field. He put us to work raking the ground. We worked for almost an hour before he dismissed us. My roommate said, "We have fifteen minutes to get back to the dormitory, dress, and go to breakfast."

Running like a crazed man, I took steps two or three at a time. Shucked my work clothes off in my room and put on my khakis. I got stymied knotting the brown tie. My thumbs got in the way. I yelped for help.

"Make a hole with your thumb. Loop one end around the hole and tighten," my roommate said, clearly disgusted with my failure. But he had the advantage of coming a week early and not being late like I was.

At breakfast, the senior student at the table scolded me, "Your tie is a mess. Fix it. Five demerits for a non-regulation tie."

"But how do I do it?" I asked. My request was answered with laughter. No one helped me. Glancing around the table I began to get the idea. After several mistakes I tied it correctly.

Prayer was said, food eaten, and off to school. Kamehameha at the time had a vocational curriculum. When you finished you could fix a car, string wires on a telephone pole, or make furniture. Our founder wanted us to become "good and industrious young men and women" and that is what the staff intended to do. Despite this orientation towards manual labor, the trustees had recently decided to educate bright students for college. These were in the A class with a handful in B.

I was assigned to C class for students designated to learn shop work. "I guess you're too dumb to go to college," my roommate said as he strutted off. To make matters worse, several of the boys were two or three years older than I. They were bigger and exercised their dominance by a couple of punches in the gut saying, "Eh brah. Don't be smart and make us look bad."

This is the *alamihi* syndrome that plagues Hawaiian kids. Black crabs, *alamihi*, when caught are thrown into a pail. No matter how many are in the pail, none escape. Those that crawl to the top are pulled back by captives below. With a sinking feeling I thought I'd always be at the bottom of the bucket and never get out to open windows as I had done earlier in the morning.

CHAPTER 3

The Hawaiian Language

"You can't sing Hawaiian. You can't even pronounce the words right," shouted the Reverend Stephen L. Desha. I shuffled my feet uncertain as to what to say, finally blurting out when no one in the class spoke. "We weren't taught that in public school. My parents wouldn't speak it."

Reverend Desha stared at me, his owl-sized eyes bloodshot. A diminutive man, the size and girth of a street fireplug, his hair was white and his face tan. He had a habit of shouting at you as if you had done something wrong or maybe he couldn't hear himself speak. Whatever the reason, he blasted me with, "Why not?"

I shrugged.

"The answer is the law banned the teaching of Hawaiian and your parents were afraid to defy the law. But that is not right. If you boys don't learn the language it will die. Take up your hymnals and listen to me pronounce the words."

Desha began to read a *himeni* then used a piano to get the key he wanted, sang it in Hawaiian, and asked us to join in. Most of us stumbled over the words.

With a sharp rap of a stick the Reverend said, "You're terrible." For the remainder of the class time, he had us repeat the hymn, constantly correcting our pronunciation. At the end of the hour, he dismissed us saying, "It's a shame that a school with a preference for Hawaiian children does not teach the language. I'm going to talk to the principal."

"Won't do him any good," a student next to me whispered. "The higher ups still have the missionary philosophy, anything Hawaiian is bad. He's new. He'll learn what the rules are."

I am puzzled. What's the missionary philosophy and why didn't my parents teach me Hawaiian? I thought their reason for failing to do so was to keep secrets from the kids. But my friend's claim made me think that they were ashamed to be Hawaiian and wanted to hide it.

To solve this conundrum, I asked my eighth grade teacher. "Auntie," I said, everyone called her auntie because she is a wonderful person, "Why doesn't Kamehameha teach Hawaiian? Why didn't my parents teach me Hawaiian?"

Her face wreathed into a smile, and she said, "Americanization. We have many races brought to work the sugar plantations. We are part of America and we all need to speak English. Read your history book."

I read my *History of Hawaii*. It said "...thousands of Oriental children must be brought up to have the social and governmental ideals characteristic of a typical American community." There it is: we are to be Americans, not Hawaiian, or Japanese, or Chinese, or any other race, but one people. *E Pluribus Unum*, from many into one. I went to see my friend and told him what I learned.

"Don't believe a history book written by a *haole* (Caucasian). My *tutu* (grandmother) said the missionaries stopped a lot of things, speaking Hawaiian, dancing the hula, surf riding, running around naked, and making love. All that stuff is bad."

My buddy's comments raised another conundrum. The newspapers were full of an exposé of prostitution in Honolulu. They talked about the bullpen system, where a man would get naked in one room, in a second room a man and a woman had sex, and in a third room the man got dressed. The woman stayed naked all the time and that way she could service a hundred men a day. The military instituted this practice. "Good for morale of the men," they said. But how come white folks could be naked and have sex, but the Hawaiian is told that is a bad thing?

You can ask how I know about sex. My parents and the schools didn't teach me, but the soldiers who came to defend Kaua'i knew all about it. I didn't want to try it. I was told that something evil would strike me called "the clap." Once bitten you became an imbecile. "The only way to get rid of the disease is to burn your penis," a Filipino man said. He was a shriveled up guy that looked like his appendage had been cooked. I knew I didn't want to be mutilated like that.

Vexed by these puzzles I decided to investigate. I recalled on my first visit to Honolulu a year before, the line of G.I.s outside an apartment complex on River Street. The recent newspaper articles mentioned that the 'bad girl' houses were *mauka* (mountainside) of Hotel Street and in Chinatown. I figured I could easily spot them by the lines of military men waiting outside.

I convinced Donald, a friend from Kaua'i, to go exploring on the first Saturday we received an off campus pass. It's not easy to get excused for an outing. The upper classmen loved to terrorize eighth graders. Kamehameha was a military school, and the officers and non-commissioned officers were older students. They found any excuse to hand out demerits.

One of these bully guys we called Buddha. As he walked you could see layers of fat around his stomach and rear-end rolling under his khaki clothes. Whenever we engaged in close order drill, he would walk along the line saying, "You got a non-regulation face, five demerits. Belt buckle is not polished, five demerits. Shoes aren't shined, five demerits." If you got thirty demerits you were confined to campus.

Don and I escaped Buddha's terroristic tactics and caught a bus into the city. At the time, downtown Honolulu was Oriental. For several blocks east of River Street, there were shops, cafes, retail, and wholesale stores called Chinatown.

Within its alleys raw sewerage ran into gutters leading to the sea. But mixed with the nauseating smells was the sweetness of *char siu* pork, pig's feet, sweet and sour chicken, egg *foo young*, and other food. If you held your breath for long stretches to keep your stomach from heaving, you could find an old Chinese cooking in an alley and eat all you wanted of the best Chinese food on the planet.

On this first visit into town our priority was to seek whorehouses. We left the bus and walked north to Hotel Street. Don and I looked sharp in our khaki uniforms with the big blue and white "K" patch on the left shoulder.

"This is important," the O.D. said as we left campus. "In places like Damon Tract or Kaka'ako, the local boys seeing anyone in military uniform will beat them up. They leave Kamehameha guys alone."

Here was another conundrum, the soldiers I met on Kaua'i were nice guys. Why in Honolulu were things different?

As we marched along the street we made sure to stand tall and thrust out our left shoulder with the "K" patch whenever we saw a local. For the most part we were ignored, but every now and then, we got the stare.

More than once along our route Donald would say, "Somebody's giving us 'stink eye', don't look." He could really spot stink eye. Only way to handle it is to look down, be humble, and not stare back. "If you do," the O.D. had said, "Big rap job."

After several blocks I said, "I don't see any long lines."

"I do see some buildings with red tape across the doors," Donald answered.

"Something has happened," I said.

There was a news stand across the street and we went over to talk to the Hawaiian selling papers. When I got up to him, I could tell he recognized our "K" patch.

"You Kamehameha Schools," he said. "My son went to Kamehameha."

"When?"

"Before the war."

There was a reluctance to say more and I didn't press him. Donald began to speak and I interrupted fearing he would say something that would make the man cry. "What are all the houses with red tape?"

"Police crackdown. Some wahine wrote a story about the cops taking bribes so the girls could screw without getting arrested. As long as we had martial law, the military did what they wanted. Martial law ended this month and the Governor ordered the wahines arrested."

"No more whorehouses?" Donald said.

The old guy winked. "Some still around, you just got to know where to look."

"How come the police arrest only the women and not the men?" I said.

"These women are from the mainland. No locals. Arrest them and ship them back, the governor figures that will stop the prostitution. It was a sassy big mouth haole wahine from Chicago that caused all the trouble. If she just stayed in Chinatown, nothing would happen, but she sets up house in Waikiki.

It is a bad thing to do. She gets arrested and starts yelling about her rights. No shut up. She writes a book *Honolulu Harlot* to expose the corruption in this town. Really stupid. She was making $150,000 a year. Now got nothing."

"You speak Hawaiian?" I asked.

"Sure, don't you?"

"Nobody taught me. How did you learn?"

"My grandmother, she said to all of us, 'by law the public schools won't teach you Hawaiian. I will teach you, otherwise our language will die.'"

I knew the man liked us. He gave us chocolate to munch on. I wanted to ask more questions, but Donald was restless. We said goodbye and walked away. Sometime soon I would come back.

I thought of what I had learned. The law prevented the teaching of Hawaiian in public schools since the government wanted us to be Americanized. My parents wanted me to speak English for the same reason. I also suspected that being part Hawaiian and part white, they were ashamed of their native blood. That's why my dad always wore a long sleeved shirt and tie and would say to me, "You're as black as the ace of spades. Stay out of the sun."

The media talked about "the melting pot of the Pacific" where the races brought to the islands for work mixed and become one, *E Pluribus Unum*. But if we were all joined together, what would our color be? I had no answers to this.

"You're so pretty," Donald said to a teen-ager standing on the street corner by the drugstore. "Can I buy you a soda?"

The girl looked at her shoes and twisted back and forth in indecision. "I'm waiting for a friend," she said.

"That's great, my pal over there," Don shrugged in my direction, "could use a date."

"Well, maybe," the girl said.

I shook my head in disgust. I hadn't come to town to chase women. Besides I didn't have much money, only a dollar.

Another cute young lady came across the street and up to where Don and his new friend stood. The first girl said, "These two guys want to take us to the movies."

"Let's go," the second girl said.

Arm in arm, we headed for the back row of the Princess Theater.

CHAPTER 4

Wartime Honolulu

After the attack on Pearl Harbor, martial law was declared. The United States military ruled Hawai'i. Curfews, blackouts, rationing, imprisonment without trial, denial of access to the sea, and a host of other harsh actions were imposed. Japanese-American soldiers in the National Guard and ROTC were discharged from service.

There was a bright side to martial law, civil proceedings were suspended. It aided our family. My father had built the Roxy Theater in 1939. At the time, it was the largest movie house in all the islands, one thousand and fifty seats. But Kaua'i had a small population and before the war our theater was never full. By mid-1941 the bank started foreclosure, and only the coming of war halted the process.

For several years prior to the attack there were some in the military who believed that the key to conquering Honolulu was to take an outer island first before invading O'ahu. For this reason and the need to train American soldiers in jungle and amphibious warfare Kaua'i received a large contingent of soldiers from the U.S. mainland.

While these men were friendly to me, they showed resentment towards the local Japanese population. This was unfortunate, but understandable. We were losing battles throughout the Pacific and the Nazis were pulverizing the Russians.

Once America won at Midway, curfew and blackout restrictions eased. Tolerance improved, and soldiers were welcomed into our homes. The Roxy, the nearby U.S.O., bars and cafes in Kapa'a town became a focal point of food and entertainment. The aloha spirit prevailed. It's the right thing to do, take care of our servicemen. As a result enduring friendships developed.

My parents modeled their Kapa'a theater after Roxy Theater in New York City.
Our theater had 1,050 seats, state-of-the-art sound system, and a large stage with red velvet curtains. Performers like Marian Anderson performed there.
This picture shows some GIs waiting for the movie and shoeshine boys on the bottom left of the building. I was one of them.

It was a shock to learn that there was a "rap the haole" syndrome among locals in Honolulu. Areas in the town were prohibited to GIs since they were in danger of being beaten. Kaka'ako was such a place.

Without an address in Honolulu to go to and someone to be responsible for me, I could not get a weekend pass to leave campus. These facts I communicated to family in Kaua'i. It was a pleasant surprise when a distant cousin, Girlie, volunteered to take me in. I arranged for my pass and then learned that my destination for the weekend adventure would be Kaka'ako. I decided to decline, but Girlie begged me to come.

I must leave campus in uniform and return in uniform. In Honolulu I knew of nowhere to change. Trembling, I marched down the hill to the bus stop and rode in Honolulu's Rapid Transit to the drop-off point, Kawaiaha'o Church. Girlie's directions were to head into the heart of the tenement district situated between King Street and the waterfront.

I think every port city in the world must have a slum area. It stands to reason that those who land in a new country establish themselves close to the water. As the generations gain in wealth, they move away from the noise and drudgery of ships loading and unloading. What they leave behind are homes and storage facilities that are old and rundown.

In the case of Honolulu, the ancient Hawaiians loved being by the sea. But with the coming of foreigners, the whalers, the establishment of trade, and the growth of the sugar industry, the waterfront area became unwanted by all except those who are poor. The *ali'i*, Hawaiian elite, copied the missionaries and moved into Nu'uanu Valley, Waikiki, or other areas where the whites chose to live.

It's not to say that living by the sea is not desirable. But having a home by the bustling port of Honolulu is not for those who can afford to escape it. Slums by the waterfront are inevitable. Those who live in these weather-trashed homes have little hope of escaping their poverty-created prison. It is understandable that they are hostile to strangers.

I marched into Kaka'ako in my crisply starched khaki shirt and trousers, sparkling Sam Brown belt, shoes polished to a high shine, tan tie properly knotted, and my overseas cap tilted at an angle. This is the look required when you left Kamehameha. You must be sharp to escape the critical eye of the student officers. They loved to hand out demerits and keep you grounded in school.

My heart pounded faster the further I walked. The O.D.'s warning rang in my ears as I signed out at the off campus desk.

"Going to Kaka'ako," he said, a grim look on his face. "Those guys don't like soldiers. Big time rap job. Better you stay away."

"Seeing family there," I said.

"Wearing your Saint Christopher?"

I touched my shirt feeling the tiny medal, "I got it right here."

"Maybe that and your 'K' patch might save you," the O.D. said. "We'll know where to look for you when you don't come back."

His words deflated my courage, but I decided to face the worst. I needed to get out of the confinement of school. The boys of Kaka'ako can't be as bad as sharks, I thought.

With my decision made, I marched into a shabby tenement district of tired- looking one and two story buildings. Laundry lines crossed the alleys between structures. I sensed the presence of humans, the scurrying of feet, and glimpsed wraith-like figures disappearing in the winding paths between apartments. The ground was dark earth. Trash lay everywhere. Trees, shrubs, and flowers were absent. Everything looked as if they needed a thorough cleaning and a paint job.

I checked the numbers on the buildings, looking for Girlie's place. I avoided staring at anyone who might be about. Don't give stink eye. Otherwise there will be trouble. This is hard to do when apartment numbers may be obscured by dirt or humans.

I took off my overseas cap to make me look less like a G.I. Undid my tie for that is the first thing to be grabbed in a fight. I held my left arm stiff at my side, squeezed my fist to bulge out my left shoulder and its 'K' patch. My Christopher medal swung along my chest, giving me comfort that I might be safe. The priest who blessed it said, "Always wear it. The Saint will protect you in your travels."

Prayers escaped my lips as I continued along this desolate landscape of shabby buildings, alleys filled with debris, and wind-blown dust swirling like steam in a pot. I saw no one on the streets, but I knew eyes stared at me from the tenement windows above. I wondered when and where the confrontation would come. I knew it would come for I heard scurrying like a passel of rats running on a roof.

I turned a street corner and saw a number on a dirt brown building alerting me that my destination was near. On a stairway in front of me sat a Hawaiian kid, big as Buddha, his eyes staring hard, hostile, and mean. For sure, it is stink eye. I'm not certain why Hawaiian kids tend to fat. Doctors say it is not good for the heart and causes the dreaded disease of diabetes. But, since ancient times, layers of flesh have been considered beautiful and vain women become huge.

Other boys appeared on the stairway as I trudged onward. I had been taught by spear-fishermen not to flee from sharks. They consider you prey if you do. Instead, swim into them keeping your eyes on the predator. In this instance I moved forward, but I did not lock eyes with the big kid or any of the others that appeared around him. To do so is a challenge to fight. I'm not saying I am chicken. It is to say that I wanted to make peace and not war, especially if I planned to spend a weekend in the neighborhood. There are movies where the cowboy in the white hat faces a passel of bad guys and stares them down. Unlike the Westerns I didn't have a six-gun and the numbers against me were huge.

Buddha stepped down, his gang crowding around him, blocking my way. Behind me, I sensed kids running across the street. I didn't look, for the real danger is in front. But I knew the purpose of these reinforcements were to block my escape. I knew that one of them would sneak behind me, placing his body near my feet. Then the big guy in front would shove me, I would fall, and be pummeled bloody.

It came time to look up and face the mob descending upon me and parley with them. "Hi," I said, a friendly smile on my face. I opened my hands, showing that my fists were not clenched.

"What you doing here?" fat boy asked.

"I came to see my cousin." This is important. I had to show I had a relationship with someone in Kaka'ako.

"You soldier."

"No, Kamehameha Schools, they make me wear this uniform when I leave the campus." I pointed to my 'K' patch keeping my hand movement slow and unthreatening.

"You got Hawaiian? Who your cuz?"

"Girlie."

"Girlie who?"

"Alapai."

"Nobody here by that name. You lie. We going bust you up."

I felt a body behind me. I didn't dare look. My parley had failed.

Buddha came to me, ready to shove me to my doom. I stood my ground, doing my best not to show fear. I had been in my share of fights at school, but these were one-on-one, with other boys being onlookers. In front of me is a mob eager to participate in a one-sided brawl. It had been suggested to me that if I were to be beaten, put up a good fight. Show that you are tough and not afraid. I clenched my fists ready for the inevitable.

Hey, wait you guys," someone on the fringe of the crowd yelled. "My mom's unmarried name is Girlie Alapai. She told me my cousin was coming."

The mood of the mob changed. The fat guy offered his fist. "Why you no say so from the start, brah? We think you soldier."

I could have reminded him that I had said all those things, but to do so would be disrespectful, argumentative, and show hard feelings. Instead, I pushed my clenched fist against his and said, "I'm sorry. I gave you guys trouble. We *lokahi* (peace)?"

The big guy smiled and said, "Sure brah, we make peace. Eh, you want come play football with us?"

Wow, an unexpected offer. But I wondered if I escaped one scrape only to be pummeled on the playing field. With extreme nonchalance I said, "Sure. After I say hello to my cousin I'll play."

"Ok brah. Come by the open grass near the statute."

I found Girlie's apartment on the ground floor of a two story building. It wasn't much, a common room and kitchen with a bedroom on each side. Although I called her my cousin, I have never been sure of our relationship. Girlie had taken care of me as a baby and would visit our family as I grew up. She could not afford to live in Kapa'a town and had to make do on the beach at Ko'olau.

Her husband worked at Gaspro, a company located on Ala Moana Boulevard in Kalihi. You passed by it on your way to or from the airport. The gas smell was so awful that you held your breath. The same stench filled the apartment.

In the kitchen, Girlie breast fed a baby. I pecked her cheek and said, "Hello, thanks for having me. The boys want to play football."

"Go," she said.

I raced out the door leaving my cap and tie. The air outside was filled with odors of rotting things, but it was better than the smell of the room I left.

After the Japanese attacked Pearl Harbor, students like me, were introduced to the gas mask. As part of our training we were ordered to enter into a room filled with tear gas and inhale it. Despite the unpleasant sensation, it was not as choking as what I had just experienced. Kaka'ako is not Kaua'i where the air is pure and sweet.

I found the boys at the playing field near the statute of Kamehameha the Great and across the street from 'Iolani Palace. Autos rattled down King Street blowing out clouds of burnt carbon. Not a pleasant place to play. My new friends hollered to hurry and I ran to join them. Immediately I was assigned to right tackle.

At fourteen, I was five feet ten inches in height and a hundred and thirty-five pounds. Some people called me rangy and others teased me for being scrawny, but I was surprised by the kids that I played with. They looked runty and half-starved, with bones standing out on arms and chest. It was easy to understand why the fat kid that confronted me was the leader. He was the biggest guy on the playing field.

In the huddle the play was outlined for me. "I going get the ball," the fat kid said, "and you two guys," pointing to me and another, "block for me as I come around the right side."

Simple, an end sweep with a tank to mow down the opposition. The ball was hiked, the kid in front of me was thinner than I and easily blocked, but the fat guy was as slow as a stranded whale in shallow water. He plodded along so that our opponents caught up with him and fastened onto him like bees swarming around a hive. His almost inert speed slowed as tacklers hung onto him and he fell to earth with most of the defensive team clinging to his body.

In the huddle he said, "They got to me because you guys didn't block. It's down the middle this time."

But the result was the same, the big guy moving as if in slow motion, a horde of tacklers mobbing him. No finesse, just plow into the pack and fall down. It was fun.

In the huddle, I talked about a Knute Rockne movie I saw, "Hey how about throwing a pass like they do at Notre Dame?"

There were smiles from the gang and I realized that this wasn't football but rugby without backward laterals. Piling on was the name of the game and without referees there weren't any fouls called. The scrums were pure fun.

We were interrupted in our mayhem by a kid saying, "Boat coming in."

"Let's go," everyone yelled.

"Where?" I said.

"Waterfront," the kid who called me cousin said.

"Are we going swimming?"

The kid nodded.

"No shorts."

"Go in your BVD's."

"No can do."

"Mom will find you something."

I raced into Kaka'ako no longer afraid. Spoke to Girlie who gave me a tattered pair of torn denims. I shucked my uniform, leaped into the pants, and raced out the door.

"I'll wash your clothes," Girlie called after me.

It made me feel guilty because I added to her troubles. But I wanted to be part of the Kaka'ako gang and I couldn't pass up the opportunity.

Naked, except for the shorts, I raced after my new friends toward the Aloha Tower, built before World War II as a welcoming landmark for visitors to Honolulu.

Hawaiians called the harbor area, "*Ke Awa O Kou*." Nu'uanu Stream, emptying into the sea, created deep-water channels which in conjunction with a barrier of reefs and earth two hundred yards from shore created a calm-water port where deep-drafted ships could safely anchor. Foreign fur traders renamed the area "Fair Haven", "Honolulu" in Hawaiian.

The first goods traded from the port were sandalwood. When the forests were denuded whalers arrived, seeking food and supplies. With the end of whaling due to the discovery of oil in Pennsylvania, unprocessed sugar became Honolulu's primary export. At the turn of the century, pineapple was planted on O'ahu, and within three decades Hawai'i produced eighty percent of the world's supply. The port continued to expand over the years, and by 1941 there were more than forty piers.

In the early Territorial days, America's military used Honolulu as its primary coaling and supply station. Pearl Harbor, although an excellent deep water anchorage, had a major flaw, a narrow entranceway blocked by shallow reefs.

Before World War I, Congress realized that the shortcomings of Pearl needed to be corrected and appropriated money to fix the entranceway and improve the harbor. There are many stories told of the Hawaiian gods smiting down the efforts of the Corp of Engineers for desecrating the home of the shark god. But American ingenuity overcame all obstacles and transformed the lakes into a premiere naval base which housed the American Pacific Fleet. It was the arrival of the navy and its hordes of white-clad sailors which ignited the racial-military upheavals that plagued Honolulu before and during World War II.

With these thoughts rolling around my head, I sped along the macadamized pavement. The sharpness of the stones did not bother me. My bare feet had been toughened like vulcanized rubber by the coral reefs of Kapa'a, but asthma had its effects and I arrived at the waterfront breathless.

Half-naked boys leaped into the sea, their clothes lying in heaps on the pier. Entering "Fair Haven" is the largest ship I had ever seen, but instead of gleaming white sides as advertised in travel posters it is colored grey making it less visible to prowling enemy submarines. During the early months of the war Japanese undersea vessels sunk several freighters and even a troop ship. But because of our victories at sea by late 1944, the U-boat was no longer a menace.

Below me, Kaka'ako kids tread water, their dark hair plastered around their heads, their brown eyes glinting with excitement. Several of my new friends called, "Come. We dive for money."

Cash is a reason for doing anything. But I paused. It is a long jump from the ship's landing into the sea. The wooden aprons girdling the piers nearly touched the water. The sides of the boat could smash you into them.

It isn't to say I was afraid. At home, many of us played chicken with a sugar train chugging toward a trestle where I and other friends stood. Its whistle would shriek a frightening warning of its coming. Plumes of steam would erupt from its stack. Its triangular cow catcher would knife toward us threatening to sweep daredevil children from the bridge. The first to jump into the stream seven-feet below would be dubbed chicken, like the rooster who flees from a fight. The last to jump would be the winner or maybe maimed or dead. More than once I had held my ground as the locomotive charged toward me. Never the first to dive and sometimes the last, I would leap into the stream and watch the steam engine rumble by, with the wagons it hauled filled with mounds of burnt sugar cane.

But this is not Kaua'i. This is a new experience. The ship, cruising into its landing, is thousands of tons heavier than a tiny black locomotive. Huge propellers drove it through the water. I had watched mom with an egg beater and seen how flour and milk were sucked into its blades. What would I do if drawn into the whirlpool of the churning brass fins of the ship?

"In you go," the fat kid said, seizing me by my shorts and hurling me forward.

"What's the matter, chicken?" a kid said as I surfaced.

"No, I just wanted to show you my swan dive," I answered.

"What's a swan?"

"A big white bird."

"White, then you was scared."

"Oh, shove it," I said, splashing water onto him.

There was an explosion followed by a geyser of water as the fat kid smacked into the sea. Once he surfaced he said, "Come on. Ship's not landing here. I think around the corner."

The Kaka'ako gang followed him, including me. Maybe I was considered one of them. I wondered if there were some kind of weird initiation rites, like slashing your wrists and joining them together. The Cowboy and Indian movies had that ritual. Big Indian would say, "White man, we mix our blood. Become brothers." I always watched each guy to see if they showed pain. They never did.

For a long time I thought, "They are really brave." But a friend pointed out, "Look, no blood. All fake." He was right. I began to watch the action on the screen more closely, especially the fist fights and realized nobody landed a punch.

Another interesting thing, the guy in the white hat always beat the guy in the black hat. Maybe that's why the haole was superior, they were light-skinned and we were dark. I didn't think lack of color made them better, but those I met in Honolulu acted like they were. Maybe that's why there was a "rap the haole" mentality in the city.

We swam toward the approaching ship. There were soldiers and civilians lined up along the railings of the boat. Coins began to shower down. They plunged into the water with tiny splashes. The density of the sea slowed their descent and even though my eyes smarted from the salt, I could still catch the twisting coins that fell toward the bottom. Most of them were pennies, but sometimes a nickel would come downward.

I mimicked the other boys, rising to the surface, holding up my hand with a coin held between thumb and forefinger. This resulted in more coins being thrown. Those on board the ship laughed as we scrambled over each other to dive for the money.

The ship approached the dock. I was tired of the little stuff and thought to distance myself from the pack to see if I could get a bigger reward. I extended my hand like a big league outfielder getting ready to catch a long fly ball. A red-headed soldier took up my challenge and hurled a coin. It flew beyond my reach, but not so far that I couldn't dive and see it twisting toward the bottom. Spearfishing for months had made my lungs strong and I kicked hard swimming downward after the prize.

Pressure mounted in my ears. My eyes burned. The sunlight that had brightened the surface, dimmed. I wondered if I was hallucinating from a lack of oxygen. I went deeper than I had ever gone. I could barely make out the sea bed. I heard it was forty or more feet deep. Was capturing the coin worth it?

I knew it was not copper for it had glinted in the sunlight. It was a quarter that tumbled down. I reached for it. But it escaped my over-eager grasp. My lungs protested, demanding fresh air.

I ignored the danger signs: sharp pain in my ears, the crackling sounds of popping sinuses, and blood flowing from my nose. Despite these dire warnings, I kicked hard and thrust my hand toward the tumbling quarter.

It nearly escaped my grasp, popping up through the crevice in my clenched fist. I covered the coin with my left hand and swam towards the surface. The buoyant sea water rushed me upward and I broke the surface like a breaching whale. The grey boat had eased alongside the dock. Ropes were cast onto the pier and coin tossing ceased.

At dinner that night, I sat at a long wooden table with eight children, five boys, three girls, cousin Girlie, and her husband. He had just returned from work. Although he had bathed, there still lingered about his person the smell of natural gas. I wondered if the constant exposure to the fumes might eventually suffocate him. He was big, almost six feet, and heavily muscled. His hair was short and he commented that he kept it that way, for the gas smell clung to long hair.

The meal was simple, stew and rice. That was fine with me for the food was tasty. Three of the boys had dove for coins and they jabbered about the exciting time that it was.

"How much did you boys catch?" Girlie asked.

"Between us, thirty cents," one of her sons said. "The soldiers were *manini* (stingy), only throwing pennies."

"Every bit helps," Girlie said, holding open her hand.

I watched the boys dropping their coins into her palm and realized that the people at the table were at the poverty level. Like most Hawaiians, there were too many children. That's why the *hanai* (adoption) system had developed. Overburdened families would parcel out their babies to childless couples or friends who could care for them. Better that excess children survived, rather than starved.

From my pocket I pulled out the shiny quarter, three dimes, and six pennies. I dropped them into Girlie's hand.

"No need to do that," she said.

"They are for your family. Thank you for inviting me." I closed her fingers over the money. It was all I had to give, for I was as poor as they were. But I was lucky. At Kamehameha, I had three meals a day, uniforms, a room with a bed, and recreational facilities. All my needs were met.

Girlie smiled, stood up, and deposited the coins in a large glass jar half full of pennies and nickels. My quarter lay on the top, the biggest and shiniest money in the bottle. Maybe, I thought, what I gave would pay for dinner.

One of the boys said, "I didn't know you got that much diving."

"I didn't. Whenever I go out on a weekend pass the front office gives me a dollar from my pineapple earnings. Except for the quarter and a few pennies the rest is what I could spare from my dollar."

The table settled down into conversation. The children were well-mannered and Al, Girlie's husband, kept a tolerant and gentle reign on his household. In a time past, when I lived at the Morgan's home, during the hanai period of my life, the standing rules at meals were: "speak only when spoken to, be seen and not heard." At Kamehameha, when eating, silence was considered golden.

In Girlie's house it was different, and I felt that I could ask the question that burned within me. "Why do locals want to fight haole soldiers?"

Talk halted.

"That's because they don't respect us," one of the older boys said.

"You mean they insult you," I asked.

"More than that, they treat us as if we are black people. They say get out of here, don't be seen where only white people belong."

I looked at Al. "I don't think they would insult you."

"I stay out of their way," he said.

"If there's a fight," Girlie interjected, "they throw the Hawaiian in prison and give the soldier's to the MPs. I can't have my husband in jail. One day of lost work is disaster for us."

"I read that people from the southern part of the U.S. don't like black people. Is that the reason for coming down hard on Hawaiians?" I asked.

Al smoothed his hair with the palm of his hand. "Maybe, but the military guys are hard on the Japanese and even the Chinese. They don't like Asians. Probably it's because of the war with Japan. But I think their hatred goes way back long before Pearl Harbor."

"Japanese boys from Hawai'i are fighting for America in Italy. They're heroes. How come our local *isei* and *nisei* have so much trouble here?" I said.

"I don't know. If you fought at Guadalcanal or Tarawa or the Philippines, maybe it's not easy to get rid of your dislike of the enemy. But as I said, the prejudice goes way back even before World War I."

"Is that true about Hawaiian boys too? The trouble goes way back?"

"I don't think so," Al said. "I think the big *pilikia* (trouble) started with some rape case before the war."

"Enough talk," Girlie said. "It is time for the kids to go to bed."

I offered to help clean up, but my cousin could see that I was drooping. She insisted that I go to sleep. I wondered where everyone slept in such a small house with only two bedrooms. I found out as I was laid parallel to the bed railing of one bedroom and kids were lined up one by one beside me. Once the mattress was full of children lengthwise the rest were arranged onto any open space available.

Yawning, I closed my eyes thinking of the day. I survived the stare-down, played football, dove for coins, and found out about poor people in Kaka'ako. Still unanswered is the "rap the haole syndrome" in Honolulu.

On Kaua'i, the soldiers I had met were great. Fights between locals and whites did not occur. What happened to the aloha spirit?

"It's the rape case," I thought. "That is the key." I fell asleep wondering what the word meant.

CHAPTER 5

Kamehameha Schools

Over the course of the nineteenth century contact with the western world threatened the elimination of the Hawaiian people. Hundreds of thousands died from disease and the survivors lived in poverty. These facts motivated the last royal descendant of Kamehameha, Bernice Pauahi Bishop, to give her vast land estate into trust for the purpose of establishing schools for Hawaiian children. She believed education would save her race and stated in her legacy that the schools should produce "good and industrious young men and women."

A school for boys started in 1887 to be followed by a school for girls. By World War II a vast campus had been established on Kapalama Heights. Its high place above Honolulu Harbor afforded students a sweeping panoramic view from the Wai'anae Mountains in the west to Punchbowl Crater in the east. There was only one roadway in and out which, when added to the imposing buildings, gave Kamehameha Schools the aspect of a medieval fortress on a hill.

My high school was not co-educational. Although all facilities were located on the heights, the campuses for boys and girls were separated.

The makeup of the student bodies were boarders and day scholars. Those who lived on campus came from the outer islands or rural O'ahu.

At the time I entered Kamehameha, males were trained to be blue collar workers and females to be housewives. A college preparatory curriculum was in its infancy. It reflected the dim view that the school trustees had of the educability of Hawaiians. For many of those admitted, Kamehameha was their only hope for an education.

During the 20th century, the pure Hawaiian had dwindled in numbers. Fortunately, the multitude of races that were imported to work in the sugar fields intermarried with Hawaiians. They produced mixed-blood children who could cope with the ailments visited upon the native people by foreigners. This meant that while there were some students at Kamehameha of pure blood, the majority were not.

In 1916 by act of Congress, Kamehameha instituted an ROTC program. Uniforms were provided by the U.S. and rifles. It meant that everyone at the school had clothes and shoes to wear. Of greater significance, the program gave young Hawaiians a chance to engage in a career of military service. In the plantation economy of Hawai'i there were few jobs for natives. The army provided an opportunity for graduates of Kamehameha to have an honorable profession.

The problem in a military school is that with scores of boys of various ages tossed together an inevitable pecking order will develop. It is usually the seniors and juniors against the younger guys.

"Hey, you," an older kid would holler, "clean the latrines. Mop the floors." Then there were the physical confrontations, the battles for dominance. ROTC enhanced the warrior aspect of young men and forced those engaged in learning about war to prove their masculinity.

"That is not what I want to be like," my new roommate said.

"You mean being a bully like the older guys are?" I answered.

"Yes, and the teasing and punching."

"We just have to take it."

"I can't stand it. Maybe I'll talk to the teachers."

"If you do you'll be considered a crybaby and guys will be tougher on you."

"I don't care. I can't stand this much longer. Boys are calling me "*mahu*."

"*Mahu*. What's that?"

"You don't know what it means?"

"No."

"It means you act like a female, a homosexual."

"What's 'homosexual?'"

"Look it up in the dictionary," my roommate said, exasperation written over his face.

Our conversation ended on that sour note, but I wanted to pursue the subject. I sought out the faculty member assigned to our dormitory, a handsome and athletic Chinese-Hawaiian who many of us thought of as a glamour boy. I asked him, "What's a homosexual?"

"Why are you asking me such a question?" he said.

"I didn't mean to offend you. I just heard the word *mahu* and was told it meant homosexual."

The faculty member gave me a look as if I had stabbed him in the stomach. "We don't speak of things like that. Maybe you should cleanse your mouth with soap and water and wash those words away."

"I'm sorry. I didn't know. I just wanted to find out what it meant. I apologize."

The harshness in the older man's face eased and he said, "A *mahu* is a boy who acts like a woman, but is not interested in girls, and only wants to play with young men, dismissed."

I scooted away without asking him about rape. His attitude was such that I knew he would put me on report for asking dumb questions. But his answer was not satisfying. Girls did not interest me very much. I only enjoyed the company of male friends. The young girls I knew giggled a lot and spoke to their peers behind my back. I didn't want to be the subject of female gossip. I also didn't think my roommate qualified for the definition of *mahu.*

I sought out my friend Donald who was only interested in girls. On the few occasions I went to town with him, he would march along the streets, his eyes roving, searching for willing young ladies who would return his blue-eyed stare. His single-minded pursuits were embarrassing and he earned the nicknames "wolf man" and "lover boy." Logic told me that since he only chased women he could not be *mahu.*

Donald sat in his dorm room looking at pictures. As I entered he scooped them up and hid them. "What do you want," he said, a cranky tone to his voice.

His attitude told me he had not been looking at family photos which heightened my curiosity as to what they were. But I kept my purpose in mind and said, "I want to ask you a question."

He stared at me. His color is an amazing thing, for the Hawaiians had brown eyes, dark hair and skin. Don was golden, and his eyes ocean blue. He claimed to have a quarter of the blood from a grandparent that he said was a *kahuna* (priest). Not just an ordinary witch doctor but an *ana ana*. This is the kind of shaman who prays victims to death, a very scary guy. Why had he told me this? I think it was to discourage myself and others from crossing him in anyway. Despite being Christians many Hawaiians at Kamehameha were trapped in the old beliefs.

"What's the question?" he said.

"*Mahu*. What is that?"

"Somebody call you that?"

"No way."

"Then why are you asking?"

"I heard the word and you know the old story, 'curiosity killed the cat and satisfaction brought him back.'"

"You ask too many questions about *mahu* and guys will think you're one and beat you up."

"Why do that?"

"*Mahu* means a boy that acts like a girl. If you feel that way, better hide it, or big rap job."

"I'm not a girl. Why beat somebody up for acting like one?"

"It's against the Bible, a man can't be a woman. Anyway, a queer is easy to beat up, they don't fight back."

Don's answers raised more questions. I decided not to pursue them. In grammar school it was not unusual to tease a dummy kid. It wasn't a nice thing to do, but unfortunately those who weren't bright stood out, like Fumiko. She had an animal face, a vacant look in her eyes, and slow reactions. Boys teased her and ran away laughing when she would respond with guttural sounds and feeble thrusts of her hands.

For me it was not the right thing to do. Fumiko was harmless and I realized God had not given her the gifts that many of us had. Someone told the teachers and the teasing stopped for a time. I had at least one fist fight for being a tattletale.

I never experienced a boy who acted like a girl. If *mahu* existed on Kaua'i, I was not aware of them. From a small island where both sexes lived, worked, and played together, I was thrust into an all male military school where masculinity is a requirement that is constantly tested, and femininity stands out. Being a *mahu* was not a good thing in a school like Kamehameha. I felt I needed to find out more about what the term meant and the boys afflicted by being *mahu*.

CHAPTER 6

Christmas on Kaua'i

I woke at Aunt Katie's house on my first day home for the holidays. My aunt bustled about the kitchen. She lived by the plantation clock. Every night at 8:30 she put out a kerosene lamp by her bedroom and went to sleep. Promptly at 4:30 in the morning she rose and followed the routine that had been her life for forty years, make breakfast and lunch for the workers, get out clean clothes, and be sure everyone was out the door by 5:30. The plantation had closed, her husband was deceased, but she did not break the routine.

Stepping outside into the cool brisk air, Mount Wai'ale'ale loomed deep blue. There were no clouds girdling the wettest spot on earth. It was a perfect day dry, clear and beautiful. Wai'ale'ale means 'rippling waters,' named for the pond at its top where the waters shimmer as they ripple toward the altar of god Kane placed at the edge of the dead volcano.

I had contacted my buddy Ambrose as soon as I got back to Kapa'a. He said, "Meet me at suicide bridge."

Near the edge of town, a railroad track crosses over a trestle above stream. On it, kids like me would dare a cane train to run us down. The first one to jump into the water was chicken. The last one to leap was the winner.

Mo'ikea railroad bridge today.
We would challenge the oncoming
sugarcane trains pulling cars loaded with cut cane.

(Courtesy of Kaua'i Historical Society.)

It's a stupid thing to do. A big black engine comes chugging down the track, its smoke stack spewing steam. The engine roars a fearsome noise like the Wizard of Oz made when he frightened Dorothy, the Lion, the Tin man, and Scarecrow. But the most wicked thing of all is the pointed cow catcher splayed out in front of the black engine, its iron rake ready to swipe away animals and kids foolish enough to block its path.

I biked up to the stream and saw Ambrose and another boy in the water. "What you doing?" I asked.

"Catching *opae.*"

"Why do you want shrimp?"

"We are going to fish for *oo'pu* at Ho'opi'i."

I got excited. People said it is the most beautiful swimming hole God ever made, as great as Waipahe'e and safer, no flash floods.

"Wow. Let's go."

"Wait. We almost have enough. Bobby, this is my cousin Moki."

The other kid nodded to me. He was nearly as tall as Ambrose, almost five-foot-eight and solidly built. He was so dark that some people might call him "deep purple." He had a great smile, his parted lips revealing a set of ivory teeth that sparkled in the early morning light.

After a few more minutes of poking around the rocks, Ambrose seemed satisfied with the opae they had caught and placed in a water filled jar. "Let's go."

We got on bikes and pedaled north. As the road rose upward to the lookout point, we passed the remnants of Kalakaua's sugar mill. He was the seventh ruler of Hawai'i and earned his kingship because he secured for the sugar people a reciprocity treaty with the United States. This agreement allowed importation of Hawaiian sugar to America duty-free. After its enactment in 1876 he came to Kapa'a with his cronies intending to become a rich sugar planter. They built houses and storage buildings and created a small village. But courtiers are not knowledgeable about growing sugar cane and the enterprise failed.

A smart Chinese acquired all the buildings and knew what would grow in the swamps of Kapa'a, rice. He became wealthy in the sale of that good and in buying real estate. He started the town that I lived in.

"We turn left at Hundley Hill," Ambrose yelled.

There was a parallel road below us heading toward some houses. Rumor had it that you could buy love in one of them.

Standing, we pedaled hard, crested the hill, and raced past Kapa'a School. Soon we came to what was called "Up Cannery" because it was above Kapa'a. In the 1930s independent farmers needed an outlet for their pineapple. That was why the cannery was started. It competed with the Hawaiian Pineapple Company established in my town in 1913.

A mile past the processing plant Ambrose said, "Turn right."

"This dirt road is full of weeds, guava branches over it. We're going into a jungle," I said.

"No worry. Just follow me."

That was easy for Ambrose to say for he probably had been on the trail before, but my bike lost traction and I nearly fell. "We should walk the bikes," I complained.

Ambrose and Moki did not pay attention and after several hundred yards of pedaling, they headed downhill to a slender path. I skidded to where they stood saying, "Dangerous ride."

"We leave the bikes," Ambrose answered grabbed a bag and headed downhill. I heard a distant waterfall and rushing water. My heart pounded, others had told me that Ho'opi'i was meant for fun.

The trail we followed was stunning. Ferns covered the ground on either side. Tall trees with vines of broad leafed plants twining around them rose skyward. Branches of the forest overhung the path blotting out most of the sunlight.

Emerging from the trail we saw an inviting, broad elliptically-shaped, forest pool. "How do we get down there?" I asked.

"Use those steps, or jump in. Be sure you jump far out, hidden rocks below," Ambrose said.

I thought of stories I heard of soldiers on leave diving into the sea only to crack their heads or twist their spines on submerged stones. "I'll follow you guys down." Maybe I was chicken, but I didn't intend to challenge the unknown.

We reached the pool's edge, laid down our equipment, and Ambrose opened the jar of squirming shrimp. He reached in, got one, bit its head off, pealed the body shell and baited his hook. He began fishing for *o'opu*.

The technical name of this species of fish is gobie. There are thousands of varieties in the world, Hawai'i has about thirty. The o'opu begins life when eggs hatch in a fresh water stream and the larvae drift to the sea. In the ocean, the little fish spend six months growing before nature impels the adults to head upstream to their original home. It is said that in their struggle, they can swim through rapids and climb waterfalls up to a thousand feet. Like salmon, they live in fresh water for awhile, reproduce, and repeat the cycle of life all over again.

I bit into a shrimp and thought of the friendship between it and the gobie. It is not unusual to find the fish sitting like a snake by a hole in the reef. There will be tiny antennae protruding from the hiding place. On approaching the fish's lair, it will scurry inside and the antennae will disappear. It's like the gobie is on guard duty for the nearly blind shrimp.

Baiting my hook, I heard Ambrose say, "No fish, let's go further downstream."

"Maybe this is the wrong time," I answered. "O'opu season is in the early fall when rain washes them to the sea."

"No, we can catch them anytime," Ambrose said as he hauled in a wriggler. He grasped the slimy fish by the gills to remove the hook and dropped it into a bag by his side.

My light bamboo pole wobbled up and down like a leafy twig in the wind. I hauled in a fish.

Our group worked the stream, using our supply of opae. "This is the most fun I've had in months," I said.

"How's your new school?" Ambrose asked.

"Tough. Wake up in the morning at 5:00. Rush to dress and clean your room. Someone comes to inspect it. You run half-a-mile to work growing grass, run to your dorm to change, run to breakfast, and then classes. School is out by 3:00 then you run to drill or change for sports. After that you run to dress and report for inspection followed by dinner. Then it's study time and lights out at 8:30."

"Sounds like lots of fun," Ambrose laughed.

"Not fun. You start school with one-hundred merits. You lose thirty-one and you're grounded. The older guys like to trip you up and make you late for your deadlines. That means demerits."

We heard shouts, women giggling, and loud splashes in the pond above us. "Let's go see," Moki said.

Being ahead of the other two, I arrived first and discovered two girls and two boys. They grimaced when they saw me, clearly indicating by their expressions that I intruded on their privacy. This is not the time for war, I thought.

Fortunately Moki arrived. He knew one of the boys and said, "Howzit Joe, this is my cousin Ambrose and his friend Bobby."

The boy called Joe introduced us to the rest of his group, all seventh graders from Kapa'a School. "What you guys doing?" he asked.

"Catching o'opu. We are done. Challenge you to a diving contest," Moki said, shoving Joe into the water.

The girls ganged up on Moki. Ambrose and I helped him and the last seventh grader joined in. We all went into the water with a huge splash.

We surfaced laughing and Joe said, "Let's have a real diving contest up on the ledge."

The boys climbed out of the water and hiked fifteen feet to the ledge. As I looked into the pond, I thought that it wasn't higher than the pier in

Honolulu. Ambrose had said there were hidden rocks under the surface. How far out did I have to leap?

"In I go," Joe said. He leaped out feet first and plunged into the pond with his arms flailing and his buttocks breaking the surface first. The girls had declined to compete and sat on the rocks below. They giggled, shook their heads, and didn't clap as Joe bobbed up from the water.

Ambrose followed with a semi-belly-flop which brought on more laughter. I tried to do a swan dive. Hands stiff at the side, a leap up and out with arms spread out like a bird in flight, feet tucked in. I felt like a man on a cross. I paid for this bravado as the right side of my face scraped a rock and my knees banged into stone. I didn't think the girls would give me any style points and they didn't.

Moki was the best. He backed up on the ledge as far as he could, ran, and leaped out. He soared so far in the air that I thought he would smash onto the other side of the pond. He entered the water head first with his hands extended creating a minimal splash. The girls clapped and cheered and he was the winner.

After that we played "keep away" which was a lot of rough-housing. I noticed that the girls came in for their share of groping and most interesting of all they groped back.

Joe brought the horseplay to a stop when he announced, "Let's have a race, only the boys. We go from one end of the pond to the other. The winner gets to kiss Lei."

I didn't think that was much of a prize. The girl wasn't bad looking, but she wasn't pretty either. Besides she was plump, giggled a lot, and only a seventh grader. This was a contest to lose.

All five boys lined up along the rocks at the south end of the pond. Ninety feet away was the north side. Shallow rocks along its far edge added hidden danger to the challenge. I felt burning on my cheek and slight pain in my knees. This was not time to add to my woes by swimming into far away rocks. Lose, that's the answer. A kiss wasn't worth it.

A rhythmic clapping and cheers came from the girls sitting on a boulder. All hoopla intended to stir our warrior spirit. Build morale. Encourage one of us to win the prize. Who cares? Losing is my only option. The clapping stopped, followed by a slow chant of, "One, two, three, go."

Leaping out, I slipped past the rocks on the near edge. Then a slow rhythmic stroke, breathe on the left, turn and blow into the water, then left, breathe, turn and blow. I tried to see ahead, but without goggles it was difficult. I thought I heard splashing in front of me and I figured I was losing, great. My kicks and strokes slowed. Let Ambrose or Moki win.

Sensing rocks ahead, I came up smoothly over shallow, flat stones on the other side.

But where are the other guys? They were behind me!

Joe yelled, "You won."

A set up, I thought as I swam back.

Reaching them, Ambrose said, "I'm going to get a picture of you kissing Lei."

"No way," I answered.

"No pictures," Joe said. "We head to the waterfall and then Bobby can claim his prize."

We swam to where the pond narrowed and followed a slender path of water that led to an oval pool into which a fall tumbled. Swimming to it I saw that the water fell eight feet onto a shelf, washed over it, and splashed onto a shell shaped bowl poised three feet above the small pool's surface, a stunning throne to sit on.

Entranced, I hesitated in my swim, admiring the beauty of the place. There was blue sky overhead, trees bending near the water, ferns dripping down the sides of the rocks, and a few scattered flowers along the pool's edges. God had made this place for love.

Lei pushed up onto the bowl beneath the waterfall, the falling liquid sparkling in the late noon sun. The guys shoved me up onto the rock near her. An okay place for a first kiss, I thought, but someday I would bring someone special here to enjoy the beauty of this spot.

The smooth, shallow depression slid Lei and me together. She giggled as water splashed over our faces, cleansing our mouths.

The kids in the water started chanting, "*Lanakila, Kilakila,* kiss, kiss, kiss,"

"Oh, hell," I said. "Let's do it."

Lei moved her face away as I bent down and my lips caught her cheek. That was fine with me as I slid off the rock. "Let's go," I said.

Moki hung back and Ambrose went with me.

We left Ho'opi'i, hiked the trail, got our bikes, and headed home. The sun dipped behind the ancient volcano and shadows lengthened toward the sea. As we sped down Hundley Hill, I saw beyond the barbed wire fronting the beach, a figure on the reef pushing a wooden box before him. In his hand he held a stick.

"I thought no fishing?" I said.

"We can fish," Ambrose answered. "Martial law is over."

"When did it end?"

"October."

"We can swim and surf too?"

"Yes, if you can find a hole in the barbed wire and the sea mines don't get you."

"Mines?"

"Yeah, submarines drop them and they float around until they hit something."

"Are soldiers still guarding the beach?"

"No. A good thing too, they are gun happy. The new guys shoot at anything they see in the ocean."

We were winning the war, but danger was still present. Enemy submarines might still be in the offshore waters and our military was on edge. I recalled an alert in Honolulu in the fall. Searchlights knifed through the darkness, anti-aircraft guns flashed. Lights were ordered out, and a radio in a dorm room announced, "Enemy paratroopers are landing."

For a half-hour there was chaos, until the all clear sounded. It appears that someone had neglected to tell someone in charge that B-29s were in transit to Hickam Field. These were the aircraft that would be flown to Saipan and used to bomb Japan, like B-17s were pulverizing Germany.

"Are there any soldiers patrolling the shore?" I said as I pedaled alongside Ambrose.

"No. The beach bunkers are empty. Been that way since you left for school. The military is practicing amphibious landings on the west side where the beaches are long and wide."

This was a significant switch in training. It meant that we were preparing to attack volcanic islands, like Japan. The surprise attack on Pearl Harbor had ended any chance for a negotiated peace. Like Ulysses Grant in the Civil War, America would only accept unconditional surrender.

Knowing the Japanese Bushido doctrine which stresses honor and loyalty, the story of the 47 Ronin, and the Oriental desire not to lose face, I suspected that we were entering the bloodiest phase of the war. A D-day invasion of Japan could result in the annihilation of an entire nation and millions of American casualties.

I had seen the effects of war in the wounded soldiers being nursed at Kamehameha Schools and the sad letters from friends fighting in the Pacific. Many more deaths would come from the battle to conquer Japan.

I had lived my life on an isolated island, unconcerned with what happened beyond its shores. The tropical sun and soft breezes acted like an opiate that dulled the senses and made me content to accept the rules and regulations of the sugar plantation rulers of Kaua'i. We were treated to the wondrous gifts of nature like Ho'opi'i. But as I pedaled toward the lonely fisherman, trudging through the water beyond the barbed wire, I realized that our lives had changed. We were no longer an unknown savage land, but America's fortress of the Pacific, playing a vital role in winning the war.

Moanakai Road in Kapa'a area where I grew up. On the other side of the ironwood trees on the left is a lagoon protected by a volcanic reef creating "keiki" (called "Fuji" when I was a kid) beach, safe for children. There I learned to surf on an old ironing board, and used my first spear for fishing: a piece of fence wire and rubber cut from a tire tube.

The lagoon on the other side of the ironwood trees on my street. At high tide the volcanic reef on the right is often covered with water. During the war, the army placed a machine gun nest at the end of this beach and along the coastline. Barbed wire blocked beach access.

CHAPTER 7

Christmas Revelations

By December, 1944, American and British troops had chased the German army to the west bank of the Rhine River. On the Eastern Front, Russian armor and infantry crossed the Vistula River in Poland and threatened the German heartland. Victory in Europe appeared a foregone conclusion and only the insanity of Adolf Hitler kept the war ongoing.

On Kaua'i families prepared for the holidays with Christmas trees harvested from local forests. These were in short supply, and given to the U.S.O. and other places where entertainment was provided to the soldiers.

My aunt Eileen and a Hawaiian family did backyard music and hula, preparing for holiday fun. I had been taught a little of the native dance, tread with your feet, sway with your hips, and tell a story with your hands. I was never good at it, all stumbles and fumbles, but the hula done by a talented woman is a beautiful dance. Singing accompanies a hula. This is traditional since it is the *mele*, chants or songs, which tells the story of what the dance is portraying.

In ancient times, both men and women performed hula. When the Christian missionaries first observed it they condemned it as "carnality in motion." Once sugar cane became the means of wealth, the planters added their condemnation saying, "the *kanaka* won't work if they're engaged in the hula."

The dance languished until the Merry Monarch of Hawai'i, King David Kalakaua revived it. But with the overthrow of his successor Lili'uokalani in 1893 by a cabal of sugar people, the hula went into decline. It was revived in the 1930s when a Hollywood promoter used the dance to attract tourists to Hawai'i. He dressed stylishly coiffured showgirls in cellophane skirts, coconut bras, and flower leis, and had them dance during the radio show, *Hawaii Calls* or the Kodak Hula Show.

The Christian disapproval of hula dancing affected Kamehameha Schools. It was forbidden. A Hawaiian teacher proficient in the art was fired for educating students in the ancient dance. Strangely, the school for the haole kids, Punahou, founded by missionaries, made the hula part of their student performances. I know, for we arranged a talent exchange night, and the near nude, blonde, blue eyed, haole girls of Punahou danced in our school auditorium to the whooping and hollering of students. The authorities at Kamehameha banned all future exchanges and gave demerits to those of us who had arranged for such an "obscene display."

During the war years, the hula fell into decline in Honolulu. We didn't have tourists and the GIs lost interest in the performances. The girls did not strip off their skirts and bras like Gypsy Rose Lee. Besides, it was the swing era in America and jitterbugging, fast dancing, and hip songs were the rage, not slow, languorous, Hawaiian music and dance.

But those of us living in the back country and in the outer islands loved the dance. On Kaua'i we were not affected by uptight Protestant morality, for Catholics and Mormons did not suppress the native culture, but embraced it. I felt lucky that I could sing Hawaiian songs, play music with my friends, and watch my aunt and cousins dance. There is something special about interpreting the graceful movement of the hands, fingers, and hips as they tell stories of birds or gentle raindrops falling on flowers. There is too much frenzy in the rocking and jiving dances of America that displays athleticism but has no other meaning.

The holidays proved to be a special time for local boys in military service. They were granted leave to come home. Friend Jack was one of these men. Since my cousin was sweet on him, I got to visit the Hawaiian boys on the beach where there was *kani kapila*, merry music played every evening.

I screwed up my courage and asked him, "What's a *mahu* and why do people beat them up?"

Jack, who was Mormon and not a bible thumper, gave me a look like I had thrown him a curve ball that just missed hitting him, "Why do you want to know?" he asked.

"My roommate, or maybe former roommate, tells me the boys hit him because they think he is *mahu*."

"Not easy to answer you. Short story, it's a boy who thinks and acts like a girl. Now, go and play with someone else."

Jack moved away to talk with my cousin. An elderly Hawaiian sitting nearby said, "I heard you. Trouble started because Christian people claimed "the bible calls it a sin for a man to sleep with a man."

This was a new angle. A *mahu* acted like a woman, might dress like a woman, and slept with another man.

"I've slept in a bed with other boys, does that make me *mahu*?"

"Only if you play with their *olo-olo*."

"My mother and the nuns tell me never to do that. Make you sick and you will go to hell. I will not do it."

"Then you are not *mahu*."

"So why does a boy get beat up for playing with another boy?"

"In olden times Hawaiians believed that if two men or boys liked each other it was okay. But today, because of Christianity, it is not okay. So a boy who feels like a female must hide his feelings, only associate with others who are like him. If the big guys find out they pick on the person because he is different."

"I heard you became *mahu* because you were a mama's boy. You grew up without rough and tough treatment like a real man."

"Nothing to do with it, I think you born *mahu*. That's why old time Hawaiians let a boy or girl live the sex they wanted to be. But today, you better stop asking those questions, big pilikia."

His warning made me shiver. I didn't want the trouble that continued curiosity could bring a suspicion that I was *mahu*. Maybe it was best to leave the subject alone. But the answer to something else still burned inside me. "Do you know what rape is?"

Just then, guitar music sounded loud in my ears as the beach boys sitting in a half circle on the lawn began to play and sing a Hawaiian tune, "*Ahi wela mai ne loco, I ka hana, a kealoha.*" I joined in with gusto, "*E a lawe mai I ke aloha. Koni koni lua I ka pu'u wai.*"

The old Hawaiian laughed as I belted out the words.

"What's so funny," I said.

"Do you know what the song is saying?"

"No, but the melody is great. What's it mean?"

"You're telling a woman, 'I have a fire burning inside me for you. It's driving me crazy. Let me give you my aloha.'"

"What's wrong with that?"

"Nothing, but when you give a woman your love what are you doing?"

"Maybe holding her hand or kissing her on the cheek."

"More than that, you know what a rooster does to a hen or a drake to a duck when they jump on top."

I thought about that for a moment. We raised ducks and chickens and I'd seen the activity many times. "You mean when a man jumps on a woman and acts like a rooster, that is rape."

The old guy threw his head back and laughed until tears came.

"What's so funny?"

"You are a country boy. Men and women act like animals for pleasure or for children. If the woman consents to receiving aloha, it's okay. But if she says no and the man forces his aloha on her that is called rape."

Finally, I understood what the word meant. But how did rape play into the "rap the haole" syndrome that plagued Honolulu? Here was a mystery that needed unraveling.

A Hawaiian came out of his house and yelled, "Germans are beating up the Americans in France."

"You're joking," I said.

"No, for real. Radio said they're attacking in the same area where they beat the French in1940."

I immediately worried about our soldiers, especially those from the 442nd Infantry Regiment. They had taken horrible casualties in France in late October fighting to free a *Texas Lost Battalion*. The newspaper had been full of the names of dead and wounded, several from Kaua'i. "Anything about the 442nd?" I asked.

"Not in the area."

That was good news. I didn't want to see or hear about another Purple-Heart ceremony where medals were given posthumously to family members of AJAs (Americans of Japanese Ancestry) killed in action. Despite the bleak report of the fighting on the Western Front, the Pacific had become an American-controlled lake. Saipan had been conquered by June of 1944. During the course of the battle we had pulverized the Japanese navy and air force. McArthur had returned to the Philippines in October and our B-29's were fire-bombing Tokyo.

CHAPTER 8

The AJAs

I hadn't spoken to my Aunt Maggie since I returned for the holidays. She was married to Yutaka Hamamoto, a former Chairman of the Board of Supervisors of Kaua'i and one-hundred percent Japanese. The war with Japan had cost him his seat on the board and for a time placed his family in jeopardy of internment. There had been hundreds of aliens and some American citizens taken from Kaua'i to concentration camps on O'ahu. This re-location of the Japanese in Hawai'i was a trickle compared to the more than 100,000 American citizens who were moved from the west coast of the mainland and placed in guarded camps in the interior of the United States.

At war's start discrimination by the authorities had been rampant. But massive re-location was not feasible in the islands with almost forty percent of the population Japanese. The building of O'ahu as America's fortress from which the war in the Pacific would be won would have been impossible.

Despite the prejudice against them *nisei*, second generation Japanese, wanted to fight for America. President Roosevelt relented, incorporating these men into the army and allowed the creation of an all Japanese-American regiment in 1943. There were massive numbers of Hawai'i boys who volunteered. A smaller percent came from the relocation camps on the mainland. The unit created was called the 442nd Regimental Combat Team. They first saw action in Italy as part of the U.S. Fifth Army.

A few days before Christmas, I chatted with Aunt Maggie. She is short like her mother Julia, with a similar round face, pug nose, and black hair plastered around her head like a cup. "Our local boys are fighting hard against the Germans," I said.

"Yes, William," she said, with a pronounced emphasis on each word as if my name had three syllables, "We can be proud of what they have done. But we have lost many men you knew from Kapa'a: Naito, Urabe, Yamashiro, and others."

"I read that the island boys are so determined to prove their loyalty to America, they charge into blistering machine gun fire regardless of casualties."

A wry smile crossed Maggie's face. "I have heard that too. Most Japanese are small boys no taller than their rifles, but they are not afraid to fight."

"Yeah, and because of their aggressiveness these small guys put huge fear into the German soldiers. When they surrender the Germans complain, 'You're supposed to be our allies not our enemy.'"

Maggie made a wry smile. In all the time I have been with her she never laughed and was often stern, saying things like: "Have you done your homework?"

At the start of the plantation era in Hawaii the sugar owners refused to let the imported laborers bring wives. The rules were relaxed with the Japanese. Married couples contracted to work in the sugar fields. These Japanese families tended to be clannish and traditional. A member should only marry Japanese, especially the eldest son. Thus a classmate at age five was engaged to a nisei girl.

Yutaka had married a part-Hawaiian, my aunt, an act frowned upon within the Japanese community. He also had not done the traditional thing after college, move in with his family. Instead, he built a home and lived there with Maggie.

These facts prompted my next question. "These 442 boys are meeting mainland girls, Italian girls, and French girls. Do you think any one of them who gets married to a non-Japanese can bring the woman home and have a happy life?"

"I don't know if they can. The mama-san in the family runs everything. The son's wife must obey her. That is very hard to do. I couldn't live that way and didn't"

"What do you think will happen when these AJAs come back?"

"Before the war the Japanese wanted unions and to strike against the plantations."

"Yeah, I remember that, the big blue eagle and the NRA. But the men were always afraid to talk about unions when I was growing up."

"They were because the plantations would shoot strikers. They did so in Hanapepe and Hilo. When war came with martial law, you couldn't strike or have unions. Martial law is over, and I hear the talk. No more will the Japanese be considered second class citizens. Changes will happen when the boys come home."

"You're thinking that nisei boys are fighting not only to prove their loyalty but to be treated like equals when they return?"

"Yes, and bring democracy to Hawai'i."

"That's interesting. I remember a Princess Kawanakakoa speaking about a two-tiered society in Hawai'i, one for the haole and the other for the locals. You think the war has awakened a sleeping giant?"

Maggie smiled. "Well, that giant has been asleep for centuries," pointing toward Nounou Mountain which looks like a giant at rest. "We'll see what happens when the soldiers come back."

I left my aunt with lots to ponder. A *Life* magazine article I read said that relocated Japanese on the mainland were angry. Those that refused to take an oath of allegiance to America were sent to the Tule Lake internment camp. In that segregation center, Japanese men had formed a society called, "the pressure boys" loyal to Japan and desiring repatriation to that country. They had caused trouble that had to be quelled by force. In Tule, there were 18,000 adults, seventy percent of them American citizens.

Hawai'i nisei were fortunate. Most of their families had not been relocated. Those who survived the war would return to homes and places they had grown up in. They had reasons to fight not only to show loyalty, but to preserve the reputation of their families, and have an opportunity to acquire a place among the power brokers of the islands.

The Japanese boys from the internment camps who volunteered to fight had only one reason to join the army, loyalty to America. But they would not have homes to return to or communities that would treat them with fairness. It was very sad.

What would the nisei veterans do on their return to Hawai'i? We had lived our lives ruled by the plantations and the military. We obeyed orders from the top tier of elites. Could the bottom scratchers use the tools of democracy to make change?

CHAPTER 9

Waikiki

By Christmas day the Nazi attack called "the Battle of the Bulge" had been contained. There were many heroic moments during Hitler's last roll of the dice to win the war. I especially liked the story that occurred on December 21 when the 101st parachute division was encircled by the enemy at Bastogne. General von Luttwitz, the German commander, sent a message: "You are surrounded, surrender." General McAuliffe responded: "Nuts!" This answer caused a sensation at home. We cheered when General Patton broke through the German lines and relieved the trapped men in Bastogne.

After New Year's I returned to Kamehameha, determined to visit Waikiki. The military had restricted the beach from Fort DeRussy to the Moana Hotel. Martial law had ended. I believed that the public could enjoy the sea and sand like the soldiers and sailors did.

In the past much of Waikiki was swamps and stagnant ponds caused by three streams descending from the mountains into lower land. Debris emptying into the ocean from these wetlands fouled the beach and made it unsightly.

After Hawai'i became a territory reclamation efforts resulted in the Ala Wai Canal designed to divert rain water into a man-made conduit that flows into the sea. The downside was the contamination of freshwater ponds with ocean water destroying the ancient system of agriculture. The upside was the dry land available for development. It resulted in homes and hotels.

Dredging and dynamiting of coral reefs eliminated the sharp rocks that made swimming difficult. Sand was imported to make Waikiki beach broad, white, and beautiful.

Diamond Head Mountain dominates the area. That name is derived from the calcite crystals found in the crater by British sailors who mistook them for diamonds. The Hawaiian name for the dead volcano is Le'ahi. It was called that because the profile of the mountain looks like the tuna fish known as *ahi*.

Like the great rock of Gibraltar that guards the entrance to the Mediterranean Sea, the military had tunneled into Le'ahi and emplaced heavy artillery designed to fire on attacking ships. As a defense installation, entry to Diamond Head and its vicinity was forbidden.

Waikiki in the 1930s became the exclusive playground of the rich and famous. When war came it was used for rest and rehabilitation of the American military.

It took a few weeks before I found a schoolmate willing to make a field trip. The bait I used was a movie. My buddy, Donald, and I boarded a bus and headed for Waikiki.

"Look," I said pointing to the sign at Kapi'olani and Kalakaua Streets. "Kau-Kau Corner the crossroads of the Pacific."

"Yeah, and see the wooden arrows showing the way to Tokyo, Manila, San Francisco, and New York. Lots of military on the sidewalks, I don't see any locals," Donald answered.

Waikiki was filled with soldiers and sailors during
World War Two. Locals didn't feel welcome.
(Courtesy of Star Bulletin)

What he said worried me. Scores of white clad sailors strolled along the road. Interspersed among them were dozens of men in khaki. I was thin, nut brown, and wearing a pseudo military uniform. I would stick out like a lighthouse on a dark night. Donald had an advantage. He had white skin, blonde hair, blue-eyes, and a round, rosy, face like a cherub in a Renaissance painting.

"Do you want to stay on the bus and go back to Honolulu?" I asked.

Donald shook his head. "We came to see Waikiki, let's do it."

We rode past the pink building, the Royal Hawaiian, and then the oldest of them all, the stark white Moana Hotel. We got off at Kuhio Beach, the public bathing place.

Typical scene of the military barb wired
beach access in Waikiki and all beaches.

We worked our way past the barbed wire and got onto the sand. From our vantage point we could see to Fort DeRussey. A section of the beach had been cleared of obstacles and figures lay on the sand. "You think some of those guys got hit by the kamikazes?" I said.

"No, only submarine sailors stay at the hotel."

"Too bad nobody is surfing. I wanted to see the long boards in action and maybe Duke Kahanamoku."

"We owe the Duke. He brought surfing back once he became a gold medal winner."

"And he started a club in Waikiki, *Hui Nalu.*"

"Home of the Hawaiian beach boys," Donald said. "Big rivals of the Outrigger Canoe Club."

"Yeah, they competed against each other, the browns vs. whites, until they joined together."

"You told me you surfed on ironing boards."

"It was all we had. Nobody on Kaua'i could afford the big twelve to eighteen-footers they use in Waikiki. I don't understand how they maneuver those things that are as big as a rowboat."

"What about the shorter board *alaia?*"

"You can't find the koa tree to make that eight foot board on Kaua'i. The plantations cut down the forests and any other trees were chopped for cooking and heating water."

"Yeah, the Japanese love the hot bath. You tried it?"

"Best feeling in the world after work."

"Let's see the banyan court where *Hawai'i Calls* was broadcast. A movie was made about it."

I got nostalgic and began to sing *Song of the Islands* featured in that film:

> *Nani Hawai'i ka moku o Keawe*
> *Lei ha'aheo I ka Lehua*
> *A me ka maile a'o Pana 'ewa*

In the song, each of the islands has its own verses highlighting some aspect that makes it special. That's why I like it. But Donald gave me a sour look and I didn't get past Hawai'i Island in my singing. There were better entertainers than I on the weekly radio show hosted by Webley Edwards. Men like Alfred Apaka, Harry Owens, Johnny Almeida, and others who are household names in Hawai'i.

We tried to get into the Moana Hotel, but were turned away by a big guy in a white uniform. "No brown kids allowed," he said. I wondered if Donald would have made it in if I hadn't been around.

"Oh well," I said as we walked past the circular driveway that turned under a large terrace resting on white columns in front of the hotel. "I just lost my chance to be discovered as an entertainer."

"You can't sing and you're lousy on the ukulele," Donald said punching my shoulder.

I shoved him back and he stumbled out into the street. A car screeched to a stop its horn blaring.

"Hey you kids, get out of the road," the driver yelled.

"Sorry mister," I answered. Traffic was light and we hustled across the four lane roadway. Which wasn't smart, for jaywalking is a crime. But we had checked for police before crossing. There were none.

On the other side of the Moana there was a miniature golf course which didn't interest me since my dad frowned on the sport. "Boys should work and not waste time playing golf." That was his rule, work, don't play, not even football or basketball. I knew that in his time his dad did not allow him to play giving him a job from age eight on. It was tough in the old days. People had very little and only survived through what they made or grew with their hands.

As we walked toward the Waikiki Theater we passed a bowling alley, skating rink, and a bow and arrow shooting gallery. The concessions were packed with military men. Donald nudged me, "I heard about a place on Waikiki called La Lani Hawaiian Village supposed to have grass shacks, a *heiau*, luau, a volcano and the *Dance of the Fire Gods*. Let's find it."

We searched without any luck. Finally I saw an old woman whom I knew to be a local and asked her.

"Don't think it's around," she said.

"Did you ever see the show? Was it any good?" I asked.

"Hawaiians no care for it. Make us look silly."

"It was too Hollywood?"

The woman said nothing and looked away.

What she didn't say spoke volumes. Some Hawaiians did not want to be typecast as savages who lived in grass shacks, worshipped pagan gods, practiced fire rituals, and sacrificed maidens to a volcano.

We arrived at the Waikiki Theater and bought tickets to see *Bataan*, with Robert Taylor and George Murphy. The theater was not as large as my dad's Roxy, but it was beautiful with a fake rainbow bending around the screen and stage. Palm trees grew along the sides of the auditorium and painted blue clouds floated along the ceiling. The movie was a typical "gung ho" type where heroic Americans wiped out Japanese soldiers by the hundreds. The crowd cheered every time Taylor fired his machine gun.

The large military contingent in the theater and streaming along Kalakaua Avenue made me realize that the islands were not important for its agriculture, but as America's primary outpost in the Pacific. Millions were invested in barracks, bases, and structures. Soldiers and civilian workers were continually brought in to build up O'ahu. With the population of Honolulu doubled by the influx and veterans returning from horrific combat, tensions were bound to rise between locals and the military men.

There was a chilling newsreel of the battle for Saipan. Japanese civilians leaped from cliffs into the ocean. Entire families marched into the sea and drowned. Flame throwers burned enemy soldiers out of caves. There were gruesome pictures of soldiers on fire staggering out of holes in the ground.

We left the theater heading for Kau Kau Corner. "What do you think, a good movie?" I asked.

"Okay," Donald answered.

"Like Waikiki?"

"Too bad we couldn't get on the beach. But worse part no girls."

"They don't dare come here where there are two hundred guys to every female."

"Yeah, scoop up job for sure."

For a time, we walked in silence, keeping as close to the lawn edge of the sidewalk as possible. We didn't want trouble. We were vastly outnumbered.

The bridge at the Ala Wai Canal loomed ahead. A dozen old people sat on rickety platforms built over the water, fishing with long poles. I couldn't tell if they were Japanese or Chinese or both, for they wore broad-brimmed straw hats that hid their faces.

"Catching mullet," Donald said. "At one time there were clean ponds all over Waikiki. Now they must catch what is in the dirty water of the canal."

"Yeah, it used to be a great place to grow taro, rice, raise ducks, and fish. Today the land is all developed for the rich."

"Look, guy going to throw net."

At the mouth of the Ala Wai near the point where the canal reaches the ocean a dark skinned man crouched. Draped around his left shoulder were folds of mesh weighted at the bottom with lead. He studied the water and turning his hips, like a batter aiming to strike a fast ball, he threw the net into the canal. It settled into the water in a perfect circle. Once at the bottom, the fisherman hauled on a cord tied to his wrist and brought the net out of the water. Several fish wiggled in vain to escape the gilling that trapped them.

"Even the Hawaiian can't go to the sea to catch fish. To eat he must take what he can from the canal," I said.

"Time changes everything," Donald answered.

He was right. The once sleepy, friendly Waikiki was no longer a place where mom and pop immigrant could settle down and engage in agriculture. Tourists in the 1930s had caused development. The war had halted construction, but it brought hundreds of thousands of soldiers to Hawai'i, and introduced the world to an Eden.

"Once the war is over more changes will come," I said.

"Let's get a burger at Kau Kau," Donald said.

We hiked over the bridge to the drive-in. "Too crowded. Let's hit Chinatown and get back to school," I said.

We caught the bus and got transfers. Stopped off at a cheap restaurant downtown, ate, and used our transfers to get back to school. As I rode I couldn't erase the images of people jumping off of cliffs or families walking into the water to drown. Such fanaticism and refusal to surrender was unfathomable. The Japanese kids I grew up with were not that crazy. But it could be that in their home islands the Japanese were trained to obey and not think. Their choice was death and not the dishonor of surrender. I believed we were entering into the bloodiest phase of the war in the Pacific.

CHAPTER 10

School Events

It was a big day on campus, the spring parade. The entire male student body was to assemble along the roadway leading to an athletic field. We had to attend church first.

The Protestant service ended at the school auditorium with a long benediction. As I left, I passed scores of bandaged men sitting in the sun. Kamehameha's Girls School had been turned into a hospital and I wondered if these injured soldiers had fought at Iwo Jima.

Invasion of that island south of Japan, was necessary to provide an airfield for fighters to fly escort missions. America suffered 20,000 casualties to conquer it. What was more appalling was the fact that an equal number of Japanese died and few surrendered. A one-to-one ratio in combat casualties is not good. The main islands of Japan had seventy million people. If they all fought to the death as at Iwo Jima our invasion losses would be horrific.

As I hurried down hundreds of stairs to my room, I wondered if this parade was just a precursor to more deadly events like the older Kamehameha boys being conscripted into the army. It seemed a possibility, for the Germans were still fighting in Europe and the Japanese were not giving up.

After lunch I fell into ranks with my classmates. The brass on my grey uniform flashed in the blazing sun. To avoid demerits, I had cleaned my belt buckle, buttons and insignia to a golden color. You could see your face in my shoes, I had polished them mirror smooth.

Sweat ran down my neck and back in small streams. The wool clothes we wore absorbed the sun's heat like a sponge in water. I knew some of us would faint and noticed at the end of the column there was an emergency wagon ready to scoop up those who dropped out.

I said to Donald, "Grab me if I fall."

"Only if you grab me first."

Before I could answer, the company CO rattled his saber, glared in our direction, and said, "Stop talking in ranks."

I zipped my lips. He was the kind of guy who would jab his sword into your rear. It hurt and could tear an embarrassing hole in your pants.

The cadet battalion, three hundred strong, stood at attention, sweltering in the sun, waiting for orders. A kid puked lunch. It splattered on the asphalt road. The contents of his stomach sizzled on the black macadam, hot as a frying pan.

"Battalion, shoulder arms," the senior student commander ordered.

I raised my rifle that I had carved in wood-working shop, sanded and oiled nut brown onto my right shoulder. Before the war Kamehameha's cadet battalion had been armed with Springfield rifles. After the attack on Pearl Harbor every ROTC unit in the islands had their guns taken away.

Why were they taken? Possibly the weapons were needed to arm defending soldiers. But the Springfield M1903 was a bolt action five clip rifle slow to fire, and had been replaced before the war by the M1 Garand. This is an eight round semi-automatic rifle. It is a gun that can be fired by continually pulling the trigger. It is much better than the Springfield in a firefight. But I think we lost our rifles because the membership of the pre-war ROTC was Japanese and suspected of disloyalty.

"Battalion! Forward! March!"

The tramp of six hundred feet thundered the still air. The column of students stomped along the winding roadway heading for the parade ground. I tried to get the cadence right. "You had a good home when you left, your right. Jodie was there when you left, your right. Sound off, one, two. Sound off three, four. Cadence count, one, two, three, four, one-two, three-four."

I sung to myself, but without a drum I fell out of step, and had to skip to get things right. You know when you are out of step for the guy behind you hits your shoe and you trip into the boy ahead. Of course, even if you weren't out of step the bigger guy behind might kick your foot and make you stumble out of ranks.

The battalion marched onto the oval track of the field following the color guard. Each of the six companies were led by a senior officer accompanied by a female student sponsor dressed in white with a medium blue cape swirling around her shoulders and a smart white military hat covering her hair. It was an inspiring sight as we stepped smartly in front of grandstands filled with family and friends. We came to a halt in a long line in front of them. We dressed our ranks and waited for the inspection by the school president and invited military officers.

A typical Kamehameha parade of the student battalions.
I am the second from the left.

Once this occurred, we performed the manual of arms and other drills, and then passed in review. Each company marched by the spectators, keeping our files arrow-straight and turning eyes right as we marched by the grandstand filled with the special guests. The student battalion headed out of the parade field and was dismissed.

Without any family to visit with I ran to my dormitory, changed, and went into the common room to play ping pong. One of the special guests at the event was speaking to a faculty member. I heard the words, "Damon Tract."

In the past, I had learned this tenement district was the meanest in Honolulu, worse than Kaka'ako. It was adjacent to the local airport, five miles from Pearl Harbor, and near the main housing of the military on O'ahu. Haole soldiers who entered it must beware for gangs of locals took on anyone in uniform.

"Why do you want to buy in Damon Tract?" the special guest asked. "Better values in Waikiki."

"That's if you want to pay five dollars a square foot. Land in Damon Tract is a tenth of the price," the faculty member said.

"Only because nobody wants it, the locals make it miserable for any white person to be there."

"Why?"

"Place has had a long history of bad race relations. Long time ago, American sailors attacked a church located there because the minister wouldn't let the women fraternize with them. When the U.S. took over it was a place where riots occurred usually over women. Then came the *Massie* case."

"*Massie* case?"

"A navy wife claimed that five local men raped her. The admiral in charge of the naval station told his sailors to beat up Hawaiians. Damon Tract was the nearest place on the island to find them."

Startled, I missed the ping pong ball with my paddle. Rape, an unconsented sexual assault, had just been connected to the "rap the haole syndrome" and a new element introduced the Massie case.

I had no time to investigate this revelation, for preparations had begun for song contest. This is an annual event at Kamehameha, where classes at both the boys and girls school are pitted against each other in a battle of songs. There were two divisions, the eighth and ninth graders and the tenth, eleventh, and twelfth. There was a prize song for each division selected by the competition committee and a choice song selected by each class.

The greatest difficulty was that the songs were in Hawaiian and few of us had been taught the language in school or by our elders. The drive for Americanization had taken a toll in the preservation of the Hawaiian culture.

After days of preparation the big night came. The school auditorium was filled to capacity with standing room only. The boys wore khaki, the girls wore white dresses. Around their necks were colorful leis of a flower selected by the class.

It is hard to describe my feelings on that night for Kamehameha was the school of warriors named after the conqueror of the islands. His fierce face, covered by a royal war helmet of feathers is the logo of our school. Here we were in a grand auditorium competing with songs and not spears, and with our necks encircled with flowers. It was definitely not warlike or manly, and some might even consider it *mahu*.

I had heard of an adage which said, "make love not war". It seemed to me that nations were better served by competing in contests singing songs than hurling bombs against each other. The battles of World War Two were not over and I shuddered to think of the horrors to come.

We were first to sing and belted out our songs with gusto. I whispered to Donald, "We did good."

He smiled and said nothing.

All the classes sang and then it was time for joint class singing while we waited for the judges to decide. The boys were first and then the girls. Our music teacher led us in a lively Hawaiian song called: *Pehea ho'i au*. We brought the house down with applause.

Sad to say we won none of the three trophies awarded. The judges claimed we were flat on the prize song and our pronunciation was not perfect. We were consoled with the notion we would win next year or the year after. In all the history of the song contest, we were the only class that never won

There was a whimsical irony to this great event. A school for Hawaiians that refused to teach the language and was Protestant puritanical had allowed something naughty to be sung. *Pehea hoi au* is a ribald sex song.

An epilogue to the Damon Tract story: in November of 1945 thousands of soldiers and sailors descended on that tenement district and beat up every local they could find. Their reason: "We are beaten and robbed and the local police do nothing." A few years after that Damon Tract disappeared. Honolulu Airport expanded into it because of the huge influx of air travel generated by the Korean War and anticipation of jets flying tourists to Hawai'i.

CHAPTER 11

An Explosive Summer

On May seventh the war in Europe ended; Germany surrendered unconditionally. In the Pacific, fighting was fierce at Okinawa, 340 miles from Japan. Hundreds of kamikaze suicide attacks struck at American ships supporting the invasion. On land, Japanese soldiers and some civilians fought to the death rather than surrender. The toll of casualties for both sides was the highest in the Pacific war.

Kapa'a was a sparkling jewel when I returned for summer break. I had learned much while away. To paraphrase John Donne: I realized that I no longer lived on an island alone unto myself, but I was part of a larger world.

Kapa'a Waipouli amidst the mountains. Mt.Wai'ale'ale in the clouds,
the wettest spot on earth.

My hometown had been started by a king who wanted to become sugar rich. He failed because he and his cronies were not wise in the growing and processing of cane. A Chinese, who arrived at the same time as King Kalakaua, understood rice growing. In the wetlands to the west he planted and prospered. Soon other Chinese joined him and Kapa'a became a rice village.

Pineapple production began in Hawai'i in 1901. In 1913 a cannery opened in Kapa'a. Plantation workers quit their sugar jobs and came to Kapa'a to work or provide services for the employees of the new enterprise.

The cannery turned the small community into a town, and in the 1940s it reflected its immigrant roots. One side of the government road was mostly Chinese shops, Tam Kee, Hee Fat, Bong Young. On the other side,

Japanese stores Yukimura, Shido, Ozaki, and so on. Most Hawaiians were fishermen or government workers except for my dad and mom, half native and half European, who owned the Roxy Theater.

Before the war, times were hard. People in Kapa'a struggled to survive. Everyone needed to work together to make it. The aloha spirit of sharing and caring prevailed, part of our everyday lives. We left autos and homes unlocked. There were no thefts for only a few had anything to steal, and a thief had nowhere to hide. These were the best of times.

"How did you like Honolulu and Kamehameha?" my friend Ambrose asked.

"It is different. There is discrimination against Hawaiians and locals fight with the haole military."

"Why the trouble?"

"Not sure, but I'll find out. How about here?"

"Nothing but rumors, remember how the military shut down the unions and sent people to jail?"

"Right."

"Since the war is almost over, there are ILWU guys from Honolulu walking around and talking strike."

"Yeah, I read about them in Honolulu. The paper called them communists as if something was wrong. I thought the Russians were our friends."

"Let's go spearfishing," Ambrose said.

"I need to get my equipment. Barbed wire is still up. How about mines?"

"No worry. Nobody has exploded in the sea," Ambrose answered.

"See you in an hour," I said, running home to get ready.

I joined him at Waipouli beach. The barbed wire set into the rocks presented a huge obstacle. They had three years of rust turning the metal thorns dirty brown. My mom had said, "If you get poked by rusty metal you get lock-jaw and die."

We paused at the shore searching for a break in the defenses. We found an opening where someone had cut a way through. "Let's go," Ambrose said.

I headed into the gap. The most dangerous part was slipping on the smooth rocks and landing in the wire. I had images of Brer Rabbit, the tar baby, and the briar patch. But unlike the trickster bunny I wouldn't escape the iron thorns if I fell into them.

Slipping into the sea, its coolness made me shiver. The ocean in Hawai'i varies between seventy-two to seventy-six degrees all year round. But the warm sun that bakes you makes the first immersion feel like you are entering a tub of ice cubes.

"Let's swim this way," I said. We stroked into deeper water, following a channel. Its bottom was sandy with clumps of brain coral anchored to rocks. The sides of nature's conduit were encrusted with forests of red, white, and brown spines that sprouted like hundreds of nails punched through planks of wood. They were not sharp and easily broken if stepped on.

"Look," Ambrose said. "Kala."

There was a group of horned flat fish swimming in deeper water oblivious to our presence,

"Go left and I go right, but shoot fish not me."

"The same to you," Ambrose said,

I sucked in air and dove. Sea water is buoyant and difficult to force into. I stroked with my right hand pulling myself downward and kicked vigorously to move closer to the fish. At the bottom, I reached for knobs of coral and pulled myself forward. I held a tube with strands of rubber tied to it and a spear protruding from the cylinder.

It's not easy to shoot fish darting around in the sea. Fortunately, the kala were tame and didn't move fast. I drew back the spear, aimed at a wide hide of green skin, and fired. My body rose like a capped bottle to the surface.

"You hit him," Ambrose said.

I saw the fish at the bottom wriggling to free itself from the metal rod that transfixed it.

"Grab it before it finds a hole!" I yelled.

Ambrose dove, and attempted to grasp the metal shaft. But the fish whipped the iron rod through the water smashing it onto rocks.

I dove and seized the haft, running my hand up it to the leathery side of the fish. Kala do not have scales. They depend on the toughness of their skin for protection. The sharp spines at the top of the fish laced my hand.

Kala have knives, shaped like Turkish scimitars, sprouting in front of the tail fin. They are a wicked part of its defense system. The horn that protrudes from its head is round, dull, and not a problem. Why nature made it blunt I don't understand. If it was a spear like a swordfish has, we wouldn't mess with the animal.

I secured the fish to a cord attached to a float. Ambrose surfaced with another kala. I dipped my head below the surface. The small school of fish had fled. I checked the rubber tubing that propelled my sling and saw that it was worn.

"Let's check caves in the reef," I said. "Don't have the power for long range open shots."

Ambrose nodded and we began hunting in crevices at the bottom of the channel. Red fish hide in these sandy holes. The kumu have a face with two descending feelers like the whiskers of a goat. Another red fish, the u'u, shaped like a Flash Gordon rocket ship, will dart back and forth in its cave, but they always pause for a moment in one spot.

We dove many times. Our eyes roved the beautiful land under water, searching for fish, and looking out for the long grey shape with rows of teeth that could end our day in disaster.

My rubber sling broke, so I called to Ambrose, "Quitting time."

"Getting dark," he answered.

The sun had dipped behind the far side of the island. The blazing heat of afternoon cooled, the breezes were gentle, and the waves rolling in no longer foamed. It was a glorious time of day, when a sunny sky shades toward night, and nature is not angry. I missed this tranquility while in Honolulu, with its beaches covered with barbed wire and entry into the sea forbidden. In Kapa'a it was different. The war was almost won and the rules could be bent.

I took one kala and two goat fish and gave the rest to Ambrose. After I left him, I stopped at my friend's home. The family was poor and without a father. I found Pete and said, "This is for you."

His mother, a slender, overburdened woman who couldn't rub two pennies together said, "Stay, eat with us."

"Thank you, I need to get home." They were at the poverty level with eight mouths to feed, but my Filipino friends were gracious and willing to share. There weren't any social programs on Kaua'i where the government provided welfare. We took care of each other and made certain that those in need are helped. Tonight, Pete's family would be well fed. It was not right to burden them with another mouth. I promised my friend we would fish together soon and left.

Once home, I learned that workers were needed in the pineapple fields and I should report the next day. Early in the morning the labor truck came by and picked me up. My Japanese friend George was huddled by the vehicle stake fence and I moved to him, "Howzit."

George smiled, a rare thing for him to do during the war years, and said, "I'm good. You have been gone a long time."

"School in Honolulu. You okay?"

"Fine. No one calls me 'dirty Jap' anymore."

"Locals wouldn't do that."

"Military guys did."

"Maybe they stopped because lots of our Japanese boys from Hawai'i got killed fighting Germans?"

"Yes, plenty died from Kapa'a. My mama-san says don't talk about it."

I went silent, thinking about the local boys no longer with us. With their valor they had erased the stigma of disloyalty attached to our Japanese people in Hawai'i. As our vehicle motored for the pineapple fields, I said a prayer for our Nisei fighting men.

After the truck rose above the Anahola dip, the landscape changed from sugar fields to acres of spiny pineapple plants growing beneath the "Hole in the mountain".

"Do you believe the story that Kamehameha threw his war spear a hundred miles and pierced that rock?" I asked.

"I don't know. But it's good for tourists," George said.

"Yeah, along with the Menehune Ditch and fishpond. I don't want tourists. They will change the island."

"War makes change, you can't stop it."

The truck drove into a field filled with golden pineapple. Stepping off the vehicle I went to work. The fruit is a devil. There is a crown of thorns on its top, small thorns along its tough skinned body, and dripping juice escaping from its bottom. When the sun is high noon, your clothes are drenched with syrup. Sweat combines with it and produces a sickly-sweet awful smell.

Pineapple field with pickers. In my time we had to carry large, heavy, cotton bags to fill with pineapples, then transfer them into boxes. We were paid by the box. (Courtesy of Kaua'i Historical Society.)

It appeared there were fewer people in the fields as compared to the previous year. In a row next to me an older Filipino was filling his pitas bag with fruit, "Eh, *manong* (friend), what happened to all the workers?"

He said nothing.

Nobody likes to talk while working. It takes too much energy. I didn't ask any more questions.

A whistle blew for lunch break. There was no shade. Pineapple shrubs are less than four feet tall and the fields were without trees.

The old Filipino sat on a box and motioned me over. I smiled, sat down, and offered him dried fish from my two-cup lunch pail. He exchanged *adobo*, a spicy, vinegar and garlic drenched piece of chicken, hot and tasty. As he chewed on a salty piece of fish the man said, "You ask about fewer workers. Maybe it's the war, but I think plantations are getting ready. A big strike is coming."

"Yeah, I heard about the ILWU organizing," I said.

"They're going to bring down the big guys. Get more pay for the workers."

"But the plantations are strong. They have the military behind them. They can shoot people, like they did in the past."

My friend didn't answer. We sat and ate in silence and went back to work.

It was a summer of pineapple picking, fishing, and evenings playing music and singing Hawaiian songs. The draft was still ongoing and I wondered if the nisei boys conscripted into the army would fight in Japan. It would be like the Civil War with cousins, uncles, and nephews battling each other. Maybe the military would say, "The Japanese veterans have had enough."

The allies, America, Britain, and China, in July of 1945 demanded the unconditional surrender of Japan or it would face "utter destruction." Japan refused to accept the Potsdam declaration. It appeared the fighting would continue.

August's sun blistered me as I finished my last day of work. War had been part of my life for four years. I whistled the tune, *When The Lights Go On Again All Over The World"*. It's a song of hope that someday blackouts, rationing, starvation, slavery, barbed wire, ocean mines, submarines, death reports, and so on, will end. With the war ended, people could marry and raise families without fear of destruction visiting their doorstep. I wondered if future children would understand how helpless, alone, and frightened we were when the Japanese brought war to Hawai'i with their attack on Pearl Harbor.

Couldn't we just end the fighting and everyone go home? It was not possible. Potsdam had put the sword to the neck of the Japanese Empire and the empire had refused to yield despite its ally Germany accepting unconditional surrender.

"Do you think Japan will fight to the death?" I asked George as the pine-apple truck took us home.

"We don't talk about it," George answered.

I noticed a slight tremor in his voice and realized that there was agony ahead for my friend and his family. The conquest of Japan would require killing relatives and friends of many Japanese living in Hawai'i. I didn't realize that a resolution of the war would soon occur in a stunning and awful manner.

Enola Gay, accompanied by two other B-29s, the *Great Artiste* and *Necessary Evil* left Tinian Island in the Marianas on August 6, 1945. Only *Enola Gay* carried a bomb called "Little Boy."

Japanese radar picked up the flight of three planes, but did not scramble fighters, deeming the aircraft on a reconnaissance mission and not worth wasting aviation gas to attack. *Enola Gay* approached the flat, featureless landscape of Hiroshima at 31,000 feet, too high for anti-aircraft guns to reach. It was 8:15 a.m. Japan standard time when "Little Boy" was released. It exploded, sending heat, radiation, and pressure waves in all directions with a destructive force never seen before.

Seventy thousand people were obliterated immediately and almost seventy thousand more were affected by the nuclear explosion. Scores of buildings were leveled and Hiroshima became a radioactive wasteland.

President Harry S. Truman issued a press release saying, "The source from which the sun draws its power has been lowered upon the Far East." He concluded with these chilling words, "We (shall) obliterate every productive enterprise the Japanese have above ground in any city."

This promise of the total destruction of Japan was followed three days later by a second atomic bomb. "Fat Boy" dropped on Nagasaki, causing the same horrific casualties. Truman promised that there would be more devastating bombs to come.

Despite the opposition of Japanese fanatics, Emperor Hirohito broadcast to his subjects that all fighting end, otherwise "Japan would be obliterated." The formal surrender occurred eighteen days later.

The gruesome facts of the destructive power of the atom frightened us. "We could all be destroyed by one bomb," I said to Aunt Maggie at a family gathering.

She closed her eyes, "Yes, but right now, I pray for the people in Japan."

"Did Uncle Hamamoto have family in Hiroshima or Nagasaki?"

"I don't think so, but he has family in Japan."

"Where is he?"

"With his mother in Koloa. They are crying and praying for the dead."

"Does he think it was right to drop the bombs?"

"He didn't say. Japanese people will not talk about it like they have not talked about the bombing of Pearl Harbor and the roundup of Japanese."

"But our locals must feel some emotion."

"Yes, they do. But they remain silent. In the past the plantations preached against the Japanese and their allegiance to the Emperor. America has called them the "yellow peril" and interned thousands when war came. Would America drop the atomic bomb on Germany?"

My aunt's voice trailed off and she engaged in conversation with others. I was glad the war was over without millions of Americans and Japanese killed in conquering Japan. Some people might call the bombing racist. Maybe it was, but what was the alternative if the Bushido doctrine dictated: death before dishonor? I had too many soldier friends and I did not want them to die.

But our world had changed. The explosive power of the sun had been unleashed producing horrible devastation. With this new weapon could the earth be destroyed? There was talk of radiation from the bombs traveling through the atmosphere and contaminating everyone. Were we to disappear like the dinosaurs because of nuclear war?

CHAPTER 12

Wai'anae and Makaha

On the day of Japan's surrender I returned to school. Beach defenses and barbed wire were being removed from Waikiki.

School started with its inevitable grind of classes and homework piled onto drills, athletic activities, and a few special events. Rumors ran rampant that we would soon regain our ROTC status and receive Springfield .03 rifles.

I wanted to pursue the story of rape and how it played into the "rap the haole syndrome." I kept myself out of trouble to qualify for a weekend pass to Kaka'ako. To my surprise, a classmate invited me to Wai'anae.

Wai'anae enters the history books in 1793 when Captain George Vancouver recorded sailing by a sandy bay with a coconut grove and small village situated near a fertile green valley. In 1796, at a heiau in nearby Makaha Valley, King Kamehameha made his final human sacrifices before launching an invasion fleet against Kaua'i. His canoes were destroyed by stormy weather. Thousands died.

During the nineteenth century, smallpox ravaged Wai'anae. The disease wiped out the native population, leaving only a few survivors.

Due to its remoteness the people of Wai'anae-Makaha lived free-spirited and independent. Its distance from Honolulu gave it an aura of mystery and fear. During World War Two and after, it was an area to be avoided by soldiers on leave. It had a reputation similar to Damon Tract.

It is a thirty-five mile trip from Honolulu to Wai'anae. Instead of traveling by car, Roy chose the O'ahu Railroad which hauled passengers and freight to the west side of the island.

"These are hard seats," I said as I ran my hand over planks of wood.

"You want cushions? This is better than the windy dirt road where you bump, bump, bump," Roy answered.

"There is nothing to see and a herky-jerky ride," I said as the rail cars surged back and forth producing a nerve jarring click-clack, a sound your neck bones make when a masseuse twists too hard.

"No worse than riding a row boat in the sea."

"I don't know about that. This car smells and when you look out the window everything flashes by, makes me dizzy."

"Close your eyes."

"Then it will get worse."

I stopped talking and lapsed into silence watching the rows of tall green sugar cane stalks bending in the wind. Many had tassels of white flowers, each able to produce a seed that could reproduce the plant. Plantations do not use them. Instead, a mature stalk is cut into eighteen inch sections and planted in the ground. From the severed pieces, sugar plants emerge. Irrigation ditches sluice water into these new fields. After eighteen months the full grown cane is harvested and taken to the mill to be processed.

"Look at the ocean. Deepest blue I've ever seen," I said as the train exited wind-blown sugar fields and rolled along the coast line of 'Ewa Beach. "My father used to be a mounted patrolman in this place. He joined after he ran away from the Parker Ranch."

"How old?" Alex asked.

"Fifteen. He fled the ranch because he wanted an education. My grand-father put him to work at eight. He packed the mail to Hilo and back, a hundred and twenty mile round trip."

"Good rider?"

"The best."

I went silent watching the waves rolling into the shore. The coastline of West O'ahu is different from Waikiki, many rocks and large boulders interspersed among sand beaches. I had a feeling of being penned in. The apron of land the train traveled on was a narrow strip of ground hemmed in by mountains on one side and the sea on the other.

I thought of my dad riding his horse on the Hamakua coast on Hawai'i Island a place as forbidding as this. He had to be a brave kid to travel that frightening road.

Our journey ended in Wai'anae. We walked to Roy's home. I put my brown case in a spare room, changed into swim shorts, and joined my friend outside.

"Let's go spear fishing" he said.

Roy retrieved equipment from a shed and we hiked to the beach. Far to my right loomed Ka'ena Point, a low mountain that stretches toward Kaua'i. Locals or the Army Corp of Engineers had cleared the barbed wire from the beaches so no obstacles prevented us from entering the sea.

"This bottom is different," I said. "It looks like a giant hurled hundreds of boulders into the water. Where's the reef?"

"Under the sand," Roy answered.

I knew he was joking and decided to explore. I swam out to where the water tinged to blue and then dark blue. Treading, I had a view of a beautiful valley. It looked like an ancient god had taken a perfectly rounded cup, sliced it in half, and nestled it into the Wai'anae Range. Its surface was green and the valley splayed out onto a broad sand beach.

"This is a classic *ahapua'a*, a place Hawaiians loved to live in. What do you call that beach?" I said.

"Makaha," Roy answered.

"Where big waves come rolling in from the northwest?"

"Yes, thirty, maybe even sixty, feet in the winter."

"Nobody surfs it?"

"Boards are too big. Waves break quicker than at Waikiki and when they come at you, they are high."

"Yeah, I guess Waikiki is gentle compared to this. Here they rise fast, break, and pound you into the sand."

"Not easy to ride. You must go sideways along the curl."

"No way to do that with the big boards surfers use."

"You catch the waves on Kaua'i?"

"I did, using a cast-off ironing board. No money to buy a real one."

We ended our conversation and went to work. I speared a blue parrot fish and figured I had done enough for the day and swam to shore. Roy trailed along. We stepped out of the water near a rock-terraced peninsula.

"A *heiau* (temple)?" I asked.

"It's called Ku'ilioloa." Roy answered.

"A temple to the war god Ku?"

"In early times, Ku was a god of fishermen. This particular heiau was dedicated by the old Hawaiians to the study of astronomy and navigation."

"So the idol with the big mouth and teeth was not the god of this temple."

"Originally he was, but with time he got twisted around to be a god of sacrifice."

We headed home where I met Roy's dad. He had just returned from work.

"I'm real dirty," he said. "Join me for a hot bath."

This is an outstanding invitation. There is nothing better than an immersion into hot water. It relieves sore muscles and opens the pores to let the skin breath.

I gave my fish to Roy's mom and hustled to the heated shed housing the steaming tub. Roy's dad had undressed and washed grime from his body with a hose of cold water. He was a short stocky man, his hair cut short in the Japanese style. He had a thin moustache, unusual for a plantation worker. His naked skin was dead white although his face had tanned from exposure to the sun. As he stepped into the enclosed pond, vapors of condensed air rose. "Take off your shorts. Wash, and come in," he said.

I doused myself and slipped into the pool, its heat warming my skin. I immersed, and felt the soothing warmth relaxing me.

"How was work?" I asked.

Roy's dad said nothing.

I waited.

"Ah," he sighed, dousing his hair with water then smoothing it with the palm of his hand. "Very hard. Few of us."

"War is over. Many men will come back eager to work."

"Won't help. Wai'anae Plantation not making money. If strike comes next year, goodbye."

"But why walk out if you are going to lose the sugar company?"

"Got to do what the ILWU wants."

That ended our conversation. It was an early warning of what would come in 1946. Before the war, unions had been demanding more pay and better working conditions. After Pearl Harbor occurred their efforts were put on hold because of martial law. Germany and Japan had just surrendered. In Hawai'i and across America, pent-up labor unrest stood poised to erupt.

Our meal was sliced chunks of deep fried parrot fish and other good Japanese dishes like hot miso soup. I asked about Wai'anae and learned that the population was mostly Hawaiian and poor.

"It will be bad for us if the strike closes the plantation," Roy's mother said. She was a part-Hawaiian woman twice as big as her husband, kind, and had welcomed me in the traditional way, "*E Komo mai*," my home is yours.

It was a house without pretension, spare in furniture, its light brown painted floor covered with *lauhala* mats (plaited leaves). A rocking chair and two foot stools formed the seats for the parlor which melded into an open kitchen with kerosene stove, sink, a planked table, and chairs. Religion was not evident though I suspected Roy's dad may have once been Shinto.

After supper and cleanup we talked in the parlor. The family did not have a radio and there was no movie theater to go to. I asked about the fearsome image that Wai'anae people portrayed, "Your reputation is, 'outsiders beware'."

"This is a friendly place," Roy's dad said. "But you got to know somebody that lives here. Hawaiians don't like to be pushed around. That's the trouble with the haole. They think we are dumb hicks or gooks. You got to treat people with respect even if their color is different from yours."

"You mean it's safe to walk around Wai'anae?"

"Just go with somebody local. But if you are alone, be polite, no stink eye, and don't stay out late at night."

I went to bed pondering all I had learned, especially the effect skin color had on the attitude of others. I remembered the war stories of Hitler and his Nazi supermen, pure white Aryans with blonde hair and blue eyes. All others were sub-humans. Was that what we had in Hawai'i, a racial divide because of skin color?

This idea occupied my thoughts for the weekend and the train journey to Honolulu. I suspected that the answer I would come up with would define my place in Hawai'i and my acceptability in the great land beyond its shores, America.

CHAPTER 13

The Governments of World War Two

After my trip to Wai'anae, I became obsessed with why a devastating World War had been fought. I made many visits to the library and found a book about the governments of the 1930s and 1940s, fascism, communism, capitalism, and democracy.

A *fasces* is a bundle of wood sticks bound around an axe. It is a Roman word that expresses the unity of a nation that pledges itself to a leader who is militaristic, nationalistic, and racist. Hitler and Mussolini were clearly fascists.

Communism preached that all property is held in common and is to be shared according to the needs of each citizen. Labor is the ultimate value and is organized for the common advantage of all the members of a society. Maybe Stalin and his Soviet Union fit this definition.

Capitalism is a system where the means of production and distribution are privately owned and operated for profit and where workers' wages are kept at the subsistence level. This definition fit Hawai'i's plantation controlled economy and government.

Democracy is government by the people where everyone is equal and each person has rights, like freedom of speech, the press, a fair trial, and so on. America is supposed to be a representative democracy, but is there equality?

The post-war news spoke of the death of colonialism. It appeared that the crown jewel of the British Empire, India, sought its independence, very much like American colonies had sought independence from Britain in 1776. The Philippines were demanding independence from the United States, a colony acquired from Spain in 1898. In other parts of the world European colonial empires were crumbling.

Before I could finish my research I was summoned home for Christmas. My dad had returned from California to acquire and relocate surplus military houses. He also planned to organize his growing enterprises to ensure his future income, and retire permanently in San Francisco.

The holidays were consumed with house building during the day. In the evenings my two female cousins, five local friends, and I would drive to various parts of the island in a surplus army truck. We sang Christmas carols to anyone who would listen. It was great fun bouncing around in an open air vehicle, jostling into each other, and being a little naughty. People seemed appreciative that we made the effort to drive many miles to sing.

My dad pulled a Scrooge on me a day before Christmas Eve. He said, "You can't go out tonight. Riding in a truck is dangerous. You have to get up early."

His command made me angry. I was enjoying myself with friends and spreading good cheer to others during the holidays. But you didn't argue with the man or there would be dire consequences for talking back. He made it clear that he needed me to work hard, finish the carpentry, and not engage in frivolous fun.

I said to my cousins, "I can't go with you tonight or any night. Dad forbids it."

"Too bad. Sue will miss you. Couldn't you sneak out?"

They challenged me to be a man, defy authority, and go with them. They dangled the carrot of Sue in front of me. I felt like Odysseus being tempted by the song of the Sirens. But as Homer tells it, sailors who listened to their sweet melody crashed into rocks and died.

With a shrug, I resisted temptation and said, "I can't go." I knew if dad caught me sneaking out it would be the belt. In bed I listened to the caroling truck pick up my cousins next door, and trundle off. I fell asleep unhappy, not realizing my good fortune for making the right decision.

Next day I heard of the disaster. The truck driver fell asleep. His vehicle plunged off the road hurling its passengers onto the lip of a canyon. Anyone going over the edge would have fallen eight hundred feet onto a boulder strewn stream. Fortunately, no one fell over the precipice. There were injuries, but none serious. If I had been disobedient I might have been unlucky and rolled into the canyon.

Dad gave me a look that said, "See, I told you something bad would happen."

I said nothing, too proud to admit he was right. But this is only one of the many adventures I had, growing up on Kaua'i where I escaped death or serious injury.

My house building ended Christmas Eve spraying tin roofs with green paint. After the holiday I ushered at the Roxy Theater. I noticed something interesting in town. There were men in heavy boots, dark pants, and shirts with chains dangling along the side marching along the street stopping at each business.

I felt a chill for they were big, mean looking, and dressed like German storm-troopers. As I polished the metal frame holding a movie poster in the lobby of the theater, I heard metal jingle as chain links clashed into each other. I turned and saw two huge men clomping toward me. They were as frightening as my screen image of the Frankenstein monster.

"Kid," one of the men said, "where's the office?"

"Go up those stairs and the office will be in front of you."

Without a word they left me, their boots making a sinister drumming sound as they climbed the twenty steps to the second floor. My dad was working in the office. I wasn't certain of the intent of these men. Fearful for my father's safety, I followed them. I didn't know what I could do if there was trouble. Maybe yell for help or try to even the odds. But the size of the men and their chains were discouraging.

The office door was open. I heard someone say, "We're union and going on strike to end plantation feudalism."

The door to the office shut. Through the open transom above it I could hear words, "Contribution...good for business...you don't want something to happen to your theater."

This can't be real. This is Kaua'i, not Chicago or New York. I closed my eyes hoping that when I opened them, this bizarre dream would end. But it didn't. Chairs scraped, I fled downstairs, grabbed my polishing rag, and shined metal. Boots thundered on steps. Chains smashed against walls. The two big men marched into the foyer and down the street.

Before I could make sense of what just happened, my cousin ran across the street and said, "The aunties want to picnic at Poipu. Can you come?"

"I'll ask dad," I answered and raced upstairs for permission. In his office I could see he was upset. I blurted out my request. He grumbled but said, "You can go."

Aunt Maggie picked me up. With her son Joseph and two other cousins we headed south. The others would follow in another car. I thought I would find out about what I had just seen and heard. I related the story of the two men to Maggie.

"Before the war," Maggie said. "There was much trouble. Sugar workers got low wages. When they went on strike, the plantations made life miserable. Strike breakers, beatings, even shootings."

"You mean killing workers?"

"Yes. When I was young sixteen men were killed in Hanapepe."

"Didn't the police stop it?"

"It was the sheriff and his deputies who did the shooting."

"You mean the law is on the side of the plantations?"

"Maybe or maybe not I can't say for sure, but in the old days the workers usually got put down by the police."

"What happened during the war?"

"Same thing, but this time it was the military. Disloyal to go on strike. It meant jail if you did, or preached union."

"What about today, will the workers lose if they strike?"

"I don't know. There are men from the mainland coming here to cause trouble. Add to it the veterans returning. Something is going to happen."

I said nothing. My female cousins in the back seat with me chatted about the hula and playing ukulele.

We drove through a long tunnel of arching trees and headed for the sea. It was dry country with cactus trees and koa forests alongside the roadway. We swung into the public beach and unloaded our car. Already other members of the family were present, setting up a picnic area with tables, mats, and a canvas tent for shade.

Reef, up-thrust rock, and a sand bar made a wide circular barrier against the sea creating a natural salt water pond within its boundary. There was a thirty foot opening in the encircling rock. Ocean waves rushed through it. I watched a young girl standing on a surf board gliding through the break and heading for the beach.

Envy gripped me. Not because she was lithe and attractive, but she rode a long, smooth, shiny koa surfboard. It put my puny ironing board to shame. I watched her catch several waves wondering if she would get tired. Finally she ended and came onto the grass. She knew one of my aunts and they talked for a while. I got up my courage and asked, "Could I try surfing with your board?"

She gave me a look.

My heart sank.

"This is my nephew," my aunt said.

Realizing I am family, the young girl said, "Okay. Just a couple of rides then I have to go."

I took the board and paddled through the gap where the waves were three or four feet and rolling in smoothly. I caught one and felt exhilaration never before experienced as the beautiful big board rose with the wave and coasted toward shore. I thought to copy the young girl and stand, but fell off. Foam covered the board bobbing in the sea. Embarrassed, I swam after it, grasped a varnished side, and headed for deeper water.

Another wave came. I paddled gaining momentum. The wave crested, lifting the curved front of my board up. The squared rear end buried in curling foam. I breathed in holding my breath to avoid wobbling. Onto my knees watching my balance, and then rising to a crouch feeling a shaking as my weight shifted. I calmed myself. Inched my feet to correct the waver. Felt the board become steady and move smoothly with the wave. I stood. Perfectly balanced, I didn't fall.

As I handed the girl her surf board she said, "I didn't think you could do it when you fell. You were good the second time. Sorry I must go. If you want to try great body-surfing go down the beach that way."

My aunt Maggie gave a disapproving look. "Waves are too big. Your mother would scold us. You can't go."

The young girl smirked and left.

Her glance was enough to drive me to disobedience. But an older cousin saved me from wrongdoing. "I hear the surf is great down the beach. I'm heading there."

"Can I go too?" I asked my Aunt Katie, who watched over me while my parents lived in California.

"All right, don't take chances."

I followed my older cousin as he marched beside a shoreline strewn with boulders. In the distance I heard crashing water and as I got closer to the thunderous sound, I saw giant waves with spray flinging up like thousands of soap bubbles rising into the sky.

We arrived at a small curved beach protected on both sides by rock that jutted into the sea. From the deep blue a hundred yards from shore waves rose, drove inland, and smashed onto shallower water. Their thunder was awesome.

Into the water I strode. The bottom is not rock but sand, nice, smooth, and sloping toward the deeper sea. A wave crashed. I dove under it swimming into the trough beyond. Another giant curl charged me. Submerging, I pulled through the swell and into the deep.

Treading, I waited as the ocean drew back, dragging water into a building wave which became a wall of sea that rushed at me.

I kicked, paddled, and was lifted six or eight feet and shoved with massive energy towards the shore. I was unlucky, it crested, and hurled me down.

My head smashed on sand, my neck and back twisted then scraped along the bottom. Kicking, flailing my hands, I tried to surface, but the energy of the unleashed water kept me down.

Don't breathe. If you suck in water you will choke and drown. This lesson, I learned from divers. But how long could I keep my mouth shut before my lungs forced it open? There is a finite time that I could last without fresh air. That time comes when dark spots appear.

I saw the black dots. They flickered like a movie reel coming to an end. This is it. I would black out and drown. Stubborn to the last, I kept my mouth shut.

My feet scraped sand. I dug them in and leaped into fresh air. I gasped its sweetness. I became giddy as I fell back into the water. The dying wave pushed me to the shore.

Resting on the sand I began thinking about the experience. The plantations were like the giant wave, all powerful, washing over everything in its way. For scores of years they kept their workers at a subsistence level. But once the war was over, educated union men were coming from America to pull them from their submerged state and teach them that labor had great value. Maybe the big men in their dark boots and clothes are necessary to lead the way?

My escape exhilarated me. Like an addict on drugs, I went back into the water and challenged the waves. I learned my lessons: hyper-ventilating, curling my body, and avoiding the tumbling effect of the surge. What a great afternoon. Reluctantly I gave up body-surfing and joined the family.

They wanted to see the tourist attractions. First we went to Prince Kuhio's monument and park. Then to the "Spouting Horn" where ocean waves thrust through a tunnel under the reef and blew out a hole sending a geyser of salt water a hundred and fifty feet into the air. Sad to say, soon after I visited this wonder, the plantations exhibited their dominance by dynamiting nature's hole in the reef to reduce the spray. They said that the continual fountain of salt water affected the growth of the sugar fields nearby.

I left Kaua'i for Kamehameha. There was a rising belief in my mind as to why there existed a "rap the *haole* syndrome" in Honolulu. On Kaua'i we had maintained our "Aloha Spirit." Why are things different in the capitol? It would prove to be another "ism" the most destructive of all.

CHAPTER 14

The Massie Case

The search for reasons why anger exists can be long. A month passed before I acquired a weekend pass to visit with cousin Girlie in Kaka'ako. The locals accepted me as a friend. It came from treating them with respect and as equals, no matter how poor and black they might be.

On Sunday, Girlie bundled the family off to Kawaiaha'o Church. Built in 1842 with 14,000 blocks of coral reef dredged from the sea, it faces 'Iolani Palace, the former home of Hawaiian royalty. The stone church has an imposing façade of four Grecian columns and a tower clock that chimes the hours. Services are in English and Hawaiian,

I don't recall what was said but I did renew a friendship with an old Hawaiian who ran a downtown newsstand. Part of our conversation touched upon the "rap the haole syndrome."

"Don't have time to talk," he said. "Visit me at my stand any day but Sunday."

If you don't have too many demerits a Saturday pass is easy to get, but it took a couple of weeks before I could visit Honolulu. Once the electric trolley opened its doors, I headed for Kaeo's newsstand.

When he saw me, a smile wreathed his round brown face capped with short white hair. He was a tall man, maybe six-feet-two-inches in height, and big.

He reached below his news table and came out with a bottle of Coca Cola. "Cool yourself," he said.

Thanking him I said, "You were going to tell me about rapping the haole and how it got started."

Kaeo's smile vanished. His fists clenched and he looked around. No one could hear us. "You're a good kid. You treat people right."

"Thanks."

"But some white guys don't care about Hawaiians. For them, there's a color line."

"Haole have been here a long time."

"I'm not talking about the missionaries or their families. They took our land and ended the monarchy but they gave a lot back. It's the military guys who came here after annexation. To them we are black scum."

"I met some really nice guys from New York, the Fighting 69th Regiment."

"How old are you?"

"Going to be fifteen in October."

"You weren't born when the trouble started. Military guys didn't like Hawaiians when they came to build a navy base. Fights between them and locals happened. But the real kicker occurred when a navy wife named Massie claimed she had been raped. Somehow five locals got blamed."

A Japanese customer came to the stand bought a newspaper and cigar. He lit up and left.

"The guys were two Hawaiians, two Japanese, and one Chinese-Hawaiian. It was claimed the rape occurred in Waikiki. At the time, these guys were in Kalihi, twenty miles away."

"So they couldn't have done it."

"Right, but the navy admiral in charge of Honolulu claimed Hawaiians were animals, and let his men loose to beat up on local boys."

"Did the five guys get a trial?"

"Yes, and the jury hung up. That's when the navy went crazy. Officers notified Washington that white women were being raped and more would occur."

"I never heard of a white women getting raped, that's sex without consent, right?"

"Yes, and white women have never been raped by Hawaiians, it's always the other way around."

A customer came to buy a newspaper and fiddled with some candy. Anxious, I shuffled my shoes, scraping the soles along the sidewalk. My fingers drummed on newspaper, trying to annoy him. But the man wouldn't be distracted, took his time, and finally snatched a bag of peanuts. He paid and left.

"What happened after the hung jury?" I asked.

"The admiral went crazy. He was from the American south and believed there was only one way to treat blacks, lynch them. Navy men beat up one of the boys. He didn't confess. They thought he was dead and left."

"Was that the end of it?"

"No. Mrs. Massie's mother, husband, and two navy men grabbed Joe Kahahawai, beat him to make him admit the rape. When he wouldn't, they shot him dead."

"Were they caught?"

"Yes, with Joe's body in their car. They were going to dump him in the sea at the blowhole."

"What happened?"

"The killers got charged with manslaughter. The navy went crazy, wanted martial law in Hawai'i to stop the trial. It went on anyway. The mainland haole were found guilty and the governor let them go."

"I remember something about that, I heard Princess Kawananakoa talking on KGMB about one system of justice for Hawaiians and another system for haole."

"Yes, she called it a 'two-tiered system' one for us and the other for the high class. Go to the library and read about it. You will understand why Hawaiians have anger."

Kaeo was finished with his story. I thanked him and hurried off to the main library, three blocks away. What I read confirmed what he said and gave me a frightening understanding of the racism that pervaded America. This was especially true in the southern part, where black people were hated, and any suggestion of molesting a white girl resulted in a hanging. The news reports of the Massie case related that the admiral, other navy men, and mother Massie believed that locals were evil blacks and could be beaten or killed like any sub-human savage.

I wondered about the Hawaiian reaction to Joe's death and read about the *kanikau*, a wailing chant given when a person of significance dies. As all things Hawaiian, such religious acts were suppressed by the Christians. But on special deaths the natural inclination to mourn in the ancient way erupts spontaneously. It is a distinctive wail, ritualistic and emitted from the throat.

A chant arose from the people at Kahahawai's funeral that had not been heard since the death of Queen Lili'uokalani. Thousands of mixed-race mourners were riveted by the wailing, a lament that struck each one to the heart. Once the burial occurred, it rained and did not stop until the hills ran blood red. Hawaiians call it *uakoko*. It was clear that the gods wept for Kahahawai.

The news media expressed fear that the death of a Hawaiian would lead to violent reaction. Instead, Hawaiians themselves were fearful. Many had experienced deep sorrow when American sailors deposed Lili'uokalani and the islands were annexed. Would the navy impose martial law because of the rape claim and killing? Would they suppress Hawaiians further as occurred when Hawai'i became a territory?

At the time of the Massie case, violence did not occur. Local people were too accustomed to the feudal dictum of loyalty to the plantation lord.

But as war clouds built, and more military rushed to the islands, tensions between mainlanders and locals rose. It increased after the Pearl Harbor attack and the imposition of martial law on American citizens for the first time since the Civil War. The fear of military rule occurred with its suppression of rights, unionism, and free speech. But the new rules were not uniformly applied. There was a clear differentiation of treatment between locals and the haole. Past resentments generated by the Massie case erupted into "the rap the haole syndrome."

Kamaina (long-time residents) did not suffer retaliation for the brutalization of locals in the aftermath of the Massie case. Growing up, there was a color line in the islands, but local haole were not given trouble by Hawaiians. It is a fact that young haole loved Hawaiian culture, hula, song, and surfing. It is a fact that members of missionary families showed benevolence to the local people, but avoided socializing with them.

Others may differ with my views on the "rap the haole" syndrome. It is a touchy subject to discuss. But in writing a memoir of growing up in Hawai'i everything that is said cannot be sugar-coated. During the decades of the 1930s and 40s there was a troubling aspect to what was occurring in America and its territories. That aspect was racism.

CHAPTER 15

Tsunamis

After World War I, President Woodrow Wilson tried to end warfare. He proposed a League of Nations whose purpose was to ensure peace in the world. But the American Senate refused to adopt his plan. This doomed the first attempt by nations to end war.

For a decade and a half of my life, military turmoil consumed the earth. Japan invaded Manchuria in the year of my birth. From that time on warfare erupted in Asia, Africa, Europe, and the Pacific.

With the defeat of the Axis powers, the United States recognized its earlier mistake and now took the lead in forming a new convocation of nations dedicated to ensuring world peace. Representatives from fifty countries met in San Francisco and adopted a charter establishing the United Nations. This covenant was ratified by the five great powers in late October 1945.

For the first time in history, political and military leaders were put on trial for war crimes and crimes against humanity. The proceedings at Nuremberg against the Nazis and the trials to occur in Tokyo in May against Japanese leaders were touted as setting an international law framework for trying and punishing war criminals, past, present, and future.

With America victorious in war, in sole possession of the atomic bomb, and the establishment of a legal framework to prevent future wars, the days of fear in Hawai'i appeared over. In all respects the year 1946 began as the most peaceful, safe, and prosperous time for all of us.

I mentioned this to my classmate Roy. He said, "Things may be okay in the world, but trouble coming for the plantations."

"Yeah, I saw these ILWU guys on Kaua'i. I think they are all over the islands getting ready to strike."

"My father says it will be big trouble for Wai'anae. His plantation is shaky. A strike would end it. Then no work in my town."

"That would be bad. People strike for more money and plantations close. How can anybody win?"

"Dad says plantations make big profits. They should share with the workers. He's ready to retire and go fishing. He's got nothing to lose."

"But there are others who could get hurt if the plantations shut down."

"You remember during wartime each side told lies about who was winning? They called it propaganda. That's what I think is happening right now. Plantations are spreading propaganda if workers strike."

"I never thought about it that way, lying to make people believe something that is not true. You think the Big Five would do that?"

"Everybody lies to get something they want."

Our conversation ended and Roy left me with a lot to think about. The newspapers had interesting articles about what might be coming in the labor situation in Hawai'i. There was a claim that the ILWU is controlled by Communists who want to overthrow the country. But this is a puzzle for the Russians are our friends. At least that is what our government had said during the war and afterwards when the United Nations was formed and the Nuremberg trials got under way.

But are the Russians our friends? Former Prime Minister Winston Churchill gave a speech in March saying, "From Stettin in the Baltic to Trieste in the Adriatic an iron curtain has descended across the Continent." He went on to explain that all of Central and Eastern Europe had fallen under the control of the Soviet Union. He likened this rise of Communism to the Fascism that had driven the world into a great war and left it in ruins.

I was still wrestling with the political questions when a few days later, my cousin Buddy raced up to me and said, "Big wave has destroyed Kaua'i and Hilo."

"That's an April Fool's joke. Don't lie like that," I answered.

"I'm not kidding. A wave hit the north shore of all the islands this morning. It was huge. Come look at the ocean."

We ran to a curving wall along the winding road that serviced both campuses. There were other students standing by it looking to the sea several miles away. The ocean boiled like someone had lit a huge subterranean fire beneath the surface. Waves swept to the shore in long lines of foaming white caps.

Never had I seen such a sight. The ocean was not a series of swells, but walls of water rolling forward. We would learn that three tidal waves smashed into the islands between 7:00 a.m. and 7:15 a.m. sweeping inland for a half-mile or more in unstoppable tides of water. Five smaller waves followed the initial onslaught.

Immediately, I worried about family on Kaua'i. Everyone I knew lived close to the sea. I must have news, but the school authorities would do nothing more than require us to return to class and study. But that is hard to do when you are concerned for the safety of someone close to you.

News of the tsunami slowly filtered in. Scores of people had been swept out to sea. Villages on Kaua'i and the Big Island had been turned into rubble. There were bizarre stories of people seeing the withdrawing water and barren reefs walking into the shallow ocean to find fish. Then the drawn-back water rushed forward in a gigantic wall of water, fifty-five feet high engulfing those foolish enough to ignore the danger and challenge the power of the sea.

My physics teacher explained what happened. "Off the Aleutian Islands a powerful undersea earthquake bellowed water out in all directions. The wave went north ninety miles and hit Unimak Island killing everyone there. It traveled south at a speed of five hundred miles an hour. But this wave that crossed 2,400 miles of sea to Hawai'i may not be noticeable to ships at sea for it rises only three or four feet high. As it reaches Hawai'i, it slows down and draws the shoreline water into it building up to massive proportions. That is why they call it a tidal wave. Once it sucks in all the shallow water, reaching the height of a three or four story building, it rushes toward shore."

"So that is why, before the wave hits, the ocean falls back and the reefs are exposed," I said.

"That is correct. Once you see water drawing back, run for the high ground," the teacher answered.

In the days following word kept coming in of tragedies and heroic stories. None of my family were affected by the tsunami nor had we lost property, but other student families were not so lucky. The April Fools cataclysm killed 159 people and destroyed coastal buildings and homes throughout the Hawaiian Islands. Fewer than 60 civilians died during the Japanese attack on Pearl Harbor and private property damage was minor. The Tsunami of 1946 is the greatest civil disaster in Hawaiian recorded history.

Seven weeks passed before I could return home. My aunts, Maggie, Katie, Eileen, and cousin Pono took me on a tour of the devastation. All bridges in the north end of the island had been damaged by the calamity. The U.S. Corp of Engineers had put in place temporary crossings of streams and rivers. We drove past the red hill into the V-shaped valley of Kalihiwai, a once thriving fishing village.

Only one building remained standing out of the dozen shacks, shanties, stores and homes that made up the community. Wrecked structures and debris filled the valley on all sides.

"Where are the fifty people that lived here?" I asked.

"Dead, swept out to sea," Aunt Maggie answered.

"What about our family?"

"They were lucky. Our cousin woke early, saw the first wave and ran to warn people. When the second wave came, he spied one of his boats, jumped in, and surfed up the valley. The roof of the family home was sailing ahead of him with his mother on top. He rescued her before she went back to the sea," Aunt Katie said.

As she spoke, I grieved for friends I had lost, men and women I knew from my fishing days on the north shore. Too many had died because of lack of knowledge regarding seismic activity, tidal waves, and a failure to have an early warning system.

We motored into Hanalei Valley, its devastation shocking. Uprooted trees, broken buildings, huge black boulders littered the land like a gigantic battle had just concluded. "This is the end for the north shore," I said. "Who would want to re-build when such horror could occur again?"

"People come back and start again," Katie said.

"This is the time to buy, prices will be low," Pono said.

"What about the ghosts of those who died? Won't they return to haunt the place?" I said.

There was silence in the car. All of us were Hawaiian and steeped in the ancient lore of the kahuna. Sudden death, where children or adults are separated and killed, leads to the belief that the dead will return to find their loved ones.

I thought that the destruction was so widespread and the human losses so great that it was sacrilegious to rebuild on ground that was almost sacred. "Instead of homes near the water there should be memorials and crosses honoring those that died," I said.

"Even if it's dangerous, people like to live near the sea. Owners will rebuild," Aunt Maggie said.

Maybe my thoughts were foolish, because I loved living by the ocean with its cool breezes, a usually calm sea, a place to splash, swim, and play. But the destructiveness of a tsunami is awesome. How many more quakes would occur to the north? No one knew. But only in Kalihiwai did a few survivors move to the hills to live.

As we cleared the debris empathy developed for the homeless people in Europe and the radiated survivors of Hiroshima and Nagasaki. We were all victims of destruction. On every island nature's fury had left devastation and grim human losses. The year 1946 which started on a positive note of future peace became a year that none living in Hawai'i would forget.

Summer passed with sweating in the pineapple fields and a wary eye on the ocean. My labor differed from the past. Tension consumed the men, refusing to be drawn into conversation. Camaraderie disappeared. Food sharing was absent. Understandable since the lunch pails were nearly empty.

One night near the end of my vacation, I saw my friend Pete looking at the posters of the attractions to come at the Roxy Theater. "Howzit," I said.

Pete nodded his face grim, his body tense.

"Going to the show?"

"I can't," he answered shuffling his feet. "No money."

"I thought you worked in the sugar fields."

"We have a big family. My mom saves everything I make."

"Come on, I'll treat you."

Pete's lips parted in a half-smile, "I can't pay you back."

"No worry. My dad owns the theater."

"Yeah, I know," he said following me in.

We climbed upstairs to the balcony and the plush seats. I chose the front row center for it gave us a commanding view of the downstairs crowd.

"Never been here before, this is nice," Pete said.

"Why is your mom keeping all your money?"

"There's a strike coming. It could last a long time. We don't know what can happen."

"Why strike?"

"The union says we have to. Everybody has to go out at the same time."

The movie started and we went quiet. I couldn't pay much attention to the show even though there was a "Three Stooges" comedy. After it was over, I invited Pete to have a Coca Cola at Stumpy's, an open air café next to the highway.

Sipping my drink, I asked, "Why does the union want all of you out at once?"

"They call it showing solidarity. If we all go out, then the plantations must give in."

"But the sugar people could cause trouble, bring in strike breakers, use the police on you."

"Yeah, they have done that in the past, but there are some new laws. The union people think we can make it if we yell together with one voice. Only worry is if they get desperate and shoot people."

"That really happened?"

"Yeah, police shot fifty union guys in Hilo before the war."

"You're making me think that this strike could be as bad on the islands as the tidal wave."

"Something has to change. The system is not fair. It's on the side of the plantations."

We finished our drinks. Pete thanked me and left. Within a few days I returned to school. Then the "Great Hawaii Sugar Strike of 1946" was launched against the HSPA, Hawaiian Sugar Planters Association. The workers were out for seventy-nine days. When the strike was over, Harry Bridges of the ILWU announced that "feudalism has ended in Hawai'i."

Uncle Joe had returned from San Francisco and he made it a point to gather me up for a weekend. He drove onto campus in a black, four door, Ford automobile. It had a canvas top and made clacking clicking sounds as he drove to the signout desk.

He was not a tall man, maybe five-foot-six-inches. His ever-present cigar sat on the corner of his mouth, its ashes dripping onto his sleeveless white T-shirt. Suspenders framed a rotund belly that rolled over the top of his khaki pants. His grizzled face was covered with a two day growth of white beard sprouting round his cheeks, chin, and neck. His haircut, short in military fashion, made him look like a cranky old man.

"Get in," Uncle Joe said, his voice hoarse as if a frog had nestled in his throat.

Too much cigar smoking, I thought. "Where are we going?"

"Kahalu by the sea," Uncle sang the words.

We headed for the Pali roadway, a narrow two lane highway buffeted at its highest point by enormous winds. "This is where Kamehameha pushed over a native army and said '*auwe ke aloha e*,'" uncle said.

"Meaning what?" I asked.

"Too bad, goodbye, have a nice fall," Joe laughed.

The view of the windward side of O'ahu was stunning. I saw a long series of ridges and peaks cut by streams into deep fissures that fell steeply onto flat land covered with green plants. In the distance lay the ocean, sparkling and blue.

Joe drove slowly down the winding Pali roadway built on top of a ridgeline that in many places is a sheer drop to the flat land of Kailua and Kane'ohe. "Ever been to Kahuku, Haleiwa, La'ie?" he asked.

I signaled that I hadn't.

"Okay, I'll show you."

We continued our drive to the sea and headed northeast. Making conversation I asked, "What do you think of the strike?"

"It cost plantations millions of dollars and the union too. Only reason they won is everybody went out, twenty-five thousand workers plus their families-over seventy thousand people."

"Was it a good idea?"

"Union people are highest paid agricultural workers. But the strike closed a couple of plantations. O'ahu Railroad looks like it's finished, tidal wave destroyed lots of track, and strike cost them plenty."

"What's in the places we are going to?"

"Northeast end of the island is very beautiful, few people live there. Haleiwa has an airfield the only place where American fighters took off to fight the Japanese. La'ie has a Mormon Temple, first one built outside of the United States. Mormon missionaries came here right after the Christians. They think Hawaiians are a lost tribe of Israel. You'll like the temple. It's a pretty place. Kahuku Point is the most northern part of O'ahu, very rocky, but a nice sandy bay next to it. Huge waves in winter time. Plenty turtles there."

It was a long boring ride, but what I saw was very much like Kapa'a, small villages and lots of rain. Everything grew fast and green. We finished our tour and headed back to Kahalu. "You'll meet my misses," Joe said. "This is her car and we're going to her house. She likes octopus, maybe you can catch some before supper."

"How did you meet her?"

"On the boat from San Francisco. We fell in love right off the bat."

That was uncle. He would marry someone rich. The money would disappear and he would move on to find another lady with a fortune. During the war years he made tons of money selling Hawaiian goods that the family made for him.

He sold his two stores and left for San Francisco near the war's end. He had a hundred thousand dollars in a money belt. In Baghdad by the Bay Joe hired a whore, and brought her to his apartment. Her pimp coldcocked him and stole his money.

Some of the family thought Uncle Joe was through. At sixty-five years of age he was penniless and not pretty. His cigar smoking made him smell like a burnt field of tobacco. But uncle is a survivor. On the boat, he hooked up with a widowed rich Hawaiian lady. A woman he called, "the love of his life."

I equipped myself with fishing gear and headed into the ocean. The water was not deep, three to four feet. The bottom was grainy white coral. It had been dredged to secure stone for building.

As I hunted octopus I thought over the changes that had been wrought. My lifetime had been controlled by the sugar plantations and their need to make profits. The law stood on their side.

They gained wealth by acquiring cheap land from the Hawaiian kings and cheap labor through immigration. The war had put a crack in their control of the islands. Martial law and the military proved more powerful than the Big 5 companies. Hundreds of thousands of men had come from the mainland to teach us new ways of thinking. Thousands of Japanese nisei had gone off to war, and, as my aunt Maggie said, "they will come back with a desire to make change."

Change happened with the ILWU unionizing all the plantation workers and taking them out on a massive strike. The plantations had to agree to higher wages and reduced working hours, a major defeat for the HSPA.

A brown and white rubbery head loomed out of a hole in the reef. I prodded the creature with my spear. Sucker-filled legs grasped rock. The octopus intended to break out from his warren and escape. Soon a purple cloud filled the water as the animal blew out ink to blind me. My spear hand extended and skewered my prize before his dark screen hid him from view.

My spear moved along the edge of the cloud of ink. I knew the octopus sought to escape. I held firm and pulled back. Out of the water came a writhing medusa of tentacles and suckers. A black parrot-like beak gnashed in the bottom center of the animal's bulb-shaped body. It's powerful enough to crush coral or break the shell of crabs and lobsters.

I strung it onto my fish line and watched it wrap its tentacles around the body of my wooden float. It made me think of wartime propaganda of Fascists and Imperialist Japan wrapping its tentacles around the earth. They are vanquished, but is there a new octopus called Communism poised to replace it? Churchill seems to think so.

A block of multi-colored coral loomed in front of me. Its presence appeared strange in a landscape of scraped white reef adjacent to it. Something the dredges missed. On the top of a round pinnacle of calcified stone encrusted with brown sea weed rose a bulb, its color matching the moss that surrounded it. There is another prize to capture for dinner. Swimming toward it, my sudden commotion caused the octopus's head to disappear into the rock.

My eyes fixed on the spot. I searched the pinnacle. The seaweed fanned back and forth helping to hide the creature from my sight. It's nature's way of protecting its own.

An eye peered, lidless, white, with a dark orb in the center. I could not tell if it was curious or frightened. Sea creatures do not reflect emotions with their eyes like humans do. I wondered if it might be friendly. I had talked with boys from Anini Beach on Kaua'i and learned how they caught octopus with their fingers. Maybe I could try it on this one.

I retreated from the pinnacle and waited. After a time, I saw the brown bulb rising above the weeds. The creature's eyes scanned its surroundings. I swam toward it, disturbing the water as little as possible. I released my spear and floated to the octopus. It did not withdraw.

My hand reached out. My finger tickled the white and brown bulb. Its body pulsed like it knew me. I stroked its head and I watched as a tentacle eased out of the rock and began exploring my hand. Soon others joined and the octopus lay in my palm, its sucker-filled tubular legs crawling up my arm, exploring.

I smoothed over the creature with my other hand. Its body turned reddish-brown and its breathing tube pumped rhythmically like a purring cat. As crazy as it seems, I thought we could become friends, enjoying a symbiotic relationship like the gobie and opae. But this brief interlude of a joinder of creatures ended as the water buoyed my hand to the surface. Realizing its danger, the animal released its hold on my arm and squirted away. I watched it flying through the sea, its bulb head in front and its tentacles trailing behind it. Saddened, I strode out of the ocean.

A red and white halo lit the top of the Ko'olau Mountains signaling the rotation into night of the earth's elliptical ball. Ripples from my ascent from the sea rolled toward the deeper ocean. Waves did not mar the surface of the water. Other than the wake made by my travel, it lay as still as a lake.

It had been a year that started with a promise of peace. But soon it had been marred by an 'Iron Curtain' speech, a display of nature's power, and a labor strike that claimed the end of feudalism in Hawai'i.

Is it impossible for the creatures of the world to live together in a symbiotic relationship for mutual advantage? Or maybe, as Rudyard Kipling had said, "O East is East and West is West and never the twain shall meet."

With these thoughts I brought my prize to my uncle and his significant other. As I pounded it with salt to soften the octopus and make it tasty, I wished I had never caught it.

CHAPTER 16

Waikiki Surfing

Containment of the Soviet Union is necessary to stop Russia from putting all of Europe under its control, George Kennan, United States Ambassador advised Harry S. Truman. The President relayed this message to Congress. Goaded by this information and Churchill's Iron Curtain speech, the House Un-American Activities Committee (HUAC) began hearings in 1947 on Communist subversion in the United States. Hollywood felt its sting as investigations started in Los Angeles. Eventually hundreds lost their jobs in the movies and were blacklisted. Stars like Chaplin and Orson Welles left the country.

ROTC returned to Kamehameha and Colonel Harold W. Kent became its first president. He had a grand idea, take the entire student body on a trip on the O'ahu Railroad. It would be the last time the rail line would carry passengers.

School buses dropped us at the Iwilei depot. Shabby tenements bordered the railroad. My classmate, Roy, said, "Plenty whore houses here."

"How come?" I asked.

"It is by the waterfront and near Pearl Harbor."

"How much?"

"Two dollars," a student said and then added with a laugh. "Back in Captain Cook's time one iron nail bought you love."

"What did the lady get for putting out? The clap or a kid or both," Roy said.

"Clap, what's that?" I asked.

"A bad disease, it killed thousands of Hawaiians. It's God's punishment for people making out with strangers," Roy said.

Students started filing into the green wagons with whoops and hollers.

"Quiet down," the OD, Officer on Duty ordered.

"How are things in Wai'anae?" I asked Roy.

"Plantation has closed. Dad's out of a job and gone fishing."

"Many people out of work?"

"Plenty and there will be more strikes soon. The pineapple canneries are next."

"Is it the ILWU that's causing the strikes?"

"It's the fault of the plantations. They don't pay fair wages. Workers are in debt," Roy said and added, "Plantations are calling the ILWU a bunch of Communists for stirring things up."

It took some time for the train to fill up so I decided to chat with my political science teacher. Taking a seat next to him I asked, "I'm reading about the United States Congress going after Communists. I thought they are our friends?"

"Before the war they were not." The teacher said. "When we fought the Germans, they became our friends. But times have changed."

"Yeah, I read in the newspaper about the "Iron Curtain" and Ambassador Kennan warning about stopping Russia. What's the worry?"

"The Communists want to take over the world. They already have half of Europe and part of Asia. Congress believes the U.S. is next."

"Is the ILWU Communist?"

"Some people in business say they are. I don't know. Keep reading the papers as you have and you'll find out."

A sudden lurch signaled the train leaving the station. It picked up speed and chugged by Pearl Harbor. Seeing the naval base whirled my thoughts back to six years in the past.

"The newspapers have stories of General Short testifying in Congress that the surprise attack was not his fault. He says that Washington did not give him all the information they possessed about Japanese plans to go to war. What do you think?"

My political science teacher paused before answering. "There were warnings. But the Army and Navy had a rivalry. They did not share information. Short thought the Navy would do reconnaissance. So he worried about sabotage and parked his planes in the center of his airfields. Admiral Kimmel thought the Army would do recon and kept his ships unprotected in the harbor. The Navy knew the Japanese would strike with submarines before an air attack. But they failed to warn the Army when they sunk a submarine outside the harbor. There were countless communication breakdowns between the two services."

"It's suggested in the newspapers that maybe Roosevelt withheld information because he wanted to go to war with Germany."

"That's too political for me. Go watch the scenery," my teacher said in an angry tone of voice.

I rejoined Roy, worried that I had upset the man with my prying questions. Steam streamed from the locomotive. Its vapors created a screen of moisture on our carriage windows before dissipating in the warm air. We passed by Waipahu with its dense fields of pineapple. I watched men tilling rows of thorny shrubs and asked Roy, "If there is a strike do you think it will end pineapple picking for us?"

"I don't know. I heard if it happens it will be on Lana'i, the Pineapple Island. Dole owns it and the union thinks that is where the workers should walk out."

"If there's a big strike against the canneries won't that hurt our agricultural industry?"

Roy said nothing. I went silent.

We traveled west to Ka'ena Point heading north to Haleiwa. "Hey, look at the surfers. They are getting wiped out."

"Makaha is not like Waikiki where the waves are gentle," Roy answered. "In winter, the ocean is huge all the way from Ka'ena to Kahuku Point. No way can you surf."

"If we lose sugar cane and pineapple do you think tourists will come to catch waves?"

"No. Too far to travel and costs too much. Only the rich can come to Hawai'i. They want a soft life and not get beaten up by big waves."

I thought about his answer. Before the war, the Lurline and Matsonia made monthly trips to Hawai'i. They carried six hundred people each. When war came the ships were seized by the military and had not been returned to Matson. Without them there could be no tourist trade. "That's good. I don't want to have people coming here."

Roy said, "You don't like foreigners?"

"Visitors who come here change everything. Unless you're a beach boy, you can't get onto Waikiki because you're brown. There are places you can't go to. Besides, I don't want to see Kaua'i changed because of tourists and hotels."

Roy went silent.

Our train lurched into Haleiwa. Chains of the railcars made rasping sounds like the Frankenstein monster struggling to break his bindings that fastened him to a prison wall. Iron wheels screeched on rails and wagons ground into each other making sounds that pierced my ears.

We were stopping for lunch, spam sandwiches. Disgusted, I said to Roy, "This is all we ate during the war and they're still feeding us this junk."

"Make the best of it. It's cheap and fills you up," Roy answered and added, "I don't like it either, but Kamehameha costs my parents a hundred dollars a year. They couldn't afford to feed me at home for that amount of money."

I shrugged and ate my food. Back on the train I watched the scenery pass by as we headed home. I admired the ruggedness of O'ahu's north shore. Few people lived there. Since it was winter time, the waves striking the boulders and sand along the coast were huge. No human could surf in that turbulent water, I thought. Time proved me wrong for the north shore of O'ahu became the Mecca of world class surfing.

Soon after the train ride, I got a note that cousin Ramona had taken a nursing job in Honolulu. With her husband Martin, they had rented an apartment in Waikiki and I could join them for a weekend.

This is pure joy. I could visit Waikiki beach no longer protected by barbed wire. Stroll along the boardwalk. See the zoo, the aquarium, and be entertained by the Royal Hawaiian Band in Kapi'olani Park.

I made all the arrangements necessary to get a weekend pass. Not to be foiled by senseless demerits, I polished my shoes, kept my uniform crisp and clean, did my work assignments, came to classes on time, and behaved.

Saturday morning came and the sky fell. There would be room inspection by the Colonel. It would be white gloves. Demerits would be handed out for poorly maintained quarters and students confined to campus for their failures.

This is a despicable turn of events. But there is a bright hope. I did not have a roommate. Success or failure lay on my shoulders.

Kamehameha dormitory where I lived is three stories high. The ground floor is devoted to storage and recreation. Levels two and three are for living with approximately sixteen cubicles per floor. My living space was on the third floor and at the far end. It would be the last to be reviewed. This is not good, for the Colonel would have learned how others cheated to make it through his inspection.

I could hear the tinkling sound of the OD's saber as he accompanied President Kent throughout the inspection. It was his duty to note the failures that were found and issue the demerits. There were groans from the floor below. I realized that the Colonel had passed out demerits like confetti during a parade. The sounds were not good.

Footsteps echoed on the stairway leading to the third floor. The dreaded duo approached. Doors opened, muffled words were said, and I heard mournful sighs from my dorm mates. There were moments of silence and I realized that one or more of my friends had made it through their inspection. "Please, God," I prayed, "let it be me too."

Two pairs of footsteps reverberated from the walls of the hallway. The inspectors were coming. I could hear them through my open door. It was made of metal and meant to remain open at all times except for fires.

A man taller than I, by at least four inches, stepped into my room. His face was clean-shaven. He was bald like my father, but bigger and more solidly built.

I could feel his eyes surveying me from head to foot. Though I shook inside, I stood at rigid attention. My arms straight, my hands with each thumb placed alongside the seams of my trousers. My brown eyes stared ahead, not daring to look at my tormentor.

President Kent asked to inspect my hands, checking my fingernails for cleanliness. Without another word, he swept his white glove over the hood of my desk light, moved his hand across my desk, walked to my two shelves above my bureau, and continued checking for dust. He opened my closet, searched for a dirty floor by moving my second pair of shoes and pushing aside my clothes.

Drawers were opened and clothes and corners were checked for cleanliness. Then the floor under my bed was swept over by the Colonel's white glove. Finally the ordeal was over as the inspectors left my room. I did not know if I had passed or failed. But the results would soon be posted for all to know. Everyone had to remain in their rooms until the inspections were completed and the resident faculty member released us.

Footsteps paced down the hallway toward my room. My sports teacher, in charge of the dormitory, appeared at my door. My heart fell for his look was sour and it appeared I had failed inspection.

"William," he paused to give emphasis to his words. "I don't know how you did it, but your review was excellent. The Colonel said, 'You have the cleanest room on campus.' You're free to go."

I didn't do anything stupid, just said, "Thank you, sir." Grabbed my brown suitcase and headed for Waikiki.

Cousin Ramona's apartment was three blocks from the beach. I changed and rushed toward the sand and sea. Gino was to meet me near the Moana Hotel. I ran to it, but didn't dare go beyond the Greek columns at its entryway. The doorman would not let me in. Instead, I circled around the building, got on the beach, and trudged onto the famous boardwalk that led from the public area past the Moana, Outrigger Canoe Club, and Royal Hawaiian Hotel.

A magnificent blue-green ocean spread out to the horizon. Foam-crowned waves, like mounded frosting on a cake, rolled into shore. They were no more than three feet high, perfect for an amateur to learn how to surf.

Waikiki Beach with perfect waves.

I searched for Gino but couldn't find him. Diving into the water to look less conspicuous, I bathed in its warmth. It was easy to understand why people said you could play in this ocean for hours without being chilled. Body surfing proved exhilarating and after each wave ride I looked for my friend. Finally he showed up.

"Having a good time," Gino said.

"Yeah, but surfing with a board is better."

"Come, we see uncle."

We scuffed sand as we walked to a hut where I was introduced to John. Gino's relative was of medium height, maybe five foot seven inches, wiry, dark, with waves of white hair, and brown eyes that were kind and friendly. "Too bad you didn't come to the beach when tourists were around," he said.

"They wouldn't let me on in the past." I answered.

"That's because you are not one of the beach boys. But even in ancient times *He'e Nalu*, wave sliding, was for the ruling chiefs, *maka 'ainana* (commoners) like you and I couldn't do it."

"Is that why surfing is called 'the sport of kings?'"

"Maybe, but that's part of publicity. In olden times, when the high muck-mucks weren't looking, the common people surfed."

"You want to try," Gino interrupted.

"Yes, but I don't own a board."

"Ever surfed?" John asked.

"With an ironing board, I never had a big one."

"Real surfers use twelve to eighteen foot boards," John said. "But maybe we can find you an eight-footer. Come with me."

Uncle went to a rack, selected two medium length boards, gave one to Gino and the other to me. Then he started a lesson.

"My nephew will help you, but let me show you the fundamentals. Try to keep your weight in the middle of the board. If you are too far back, the wave will slide under you. Too forward and you pearl dive straight to the bottom and get whacked pretty solid."

"Yeah, and you paddle out to the waves with your hands," Gino added. "Your shoulders will get tired real soon."

"Choose a wave that is just starting to swell behind you and stroke like hell. The wave will lift you and off you go," John said.

"How about standing?" I asked. "I see all those pictures of suffers upright, their hands at the side. Sometimes I've seen acrobatics on a board. A woman held high by a man."

"You are a funny kid. Don't be a hot dog and try fancy stuff before you know how to do it. Take your time, the best wave is a high smooth one without foam and doesn't break quickly. Hawaiians call it *ohu*. Not the best wave is the long one that is breaking all at once. It is called *kakala*. With skill you can get a good ride from it."

"Thanks for the tips," I said and headed into the water.

"Gino, help Williama," John said.

In the ocean, I rolled onto the surfboard and promptly rolled off. I tried again and slipped off it.

John called from the shore, "Grasp the middle and pull yourself on. Keep steady."

I followed his advice, wobbled a bit and hung on. Gino had paddled out to sea. I pursued him, stroking with both hands while trying to maintain my balance. Once settled in a sweet spot on the board it was easy.

Gino found deep water where the waves began to swell. I joined him and waited.

A wave came charging at us. Gino hauled himself onto his craft, stroked and took off. I was slow and the surge of water passed beneath me. But another came right after it. I gripped the middle, pulled myself on, and paddled. The wave lifted me high and I charged toward shore. Desperately I hung on. Don't embarrass yourself by falling off, I thought. Miracle of miracles the wave pushed me to the beach. I rolled off my surf board. It washed up the sand and bobbed back, heading out to sea.

"Grab the board before it hits somebody," John said.

I did and without another word paddled out to sea. For hours I had hilarious fun. I fell off, dove for pearls, got whacked by the board, slid off when I tried to stand, drank water, and had red eyes from the salt. But all the troubles were worth it for when you caught a wave, stood up like a statue, and rode it to shore you felt that you accomplished something great.

With the day dwindling toward evening I trudged out of the water and headed to John sitting on the sand. He was intertwining coconut leaves into the shape of a hat.

Satisfied with his work, he offered it to me, saying, "For you Williama and your great day of surfing. I charge ten dollars for this. I give it to you free."

Williama is not a name I liked, but I didn't have the heart to correct him. John was a kind man. The type of adult who will put up with kids. If he wanted to misstate my name, so be it. I could survive.

He left and soon returned with a beer and a couple of Coca Colas for Gino and me. We sipped our drinks watching the sun setting behind the Wai'anae Mountains. "You have *aloha* for the *kai* (sea)?" John asked.

"Yes and I know that you love it to," I answered.

"It is powerful and you must treat it with respect. Despite its fierceness it allowed our people to travel long distances and find this land. Like the *aina* (land), it gives us food and it sustains us in hard times when you get nothing from the land."

"I love the ocean," I answered. "It has beauty under it and on it. Today I have had thrills that I will not forget. I cannot wait until tomorrow when I can try it again."

"I will not be here on Sunday," John said.

"Nor I," Gino added.

"Then it will be sad. Maybe I can come again."

"It's possible. But until you do always think aloha kai, I love the sea."

I left them, wondering if I would ever get back to enjoy another glorious day. My cousin scolded me when I got home for being tardy, but her anger dissipated when she heard what a good time I had at Waikiki. "You must be hungry," she said.

"I haven't eaten all day. It was so exciting I forgot."

"You have red eyes."

"I was trying to look for eels and fish underwater without goggles."

We both laughed at my foolishness. Exhausted, I fell into bed.

The next day we traveled to Kapi'olani Park to listen to the Royal Hawaiian Band. The program related the history of the band. It was founded in 1836. Its most famous bandmaster was Prussian musician Henri Berger. He was called by Queen Lili'uokalani, "The Father of Hawaiian Music," for he preserved the ancient hymns, chants, and songs of Hawai'i before the overthrow.

The conductor began the concert with a Kalakaua march and then continued with a song by Lili'uokalani. It was a warm afternoon. I watched the waves rolling into the shore and wanted to be in the surf.

But the music played was poignant. A reminder of days long past. When they did *Aloha 'Oe*, I almost cried thinking of what Hawaiians had lost when the Queen was deposed by the sugar people with the help of American Marines. The new leaders ripped our culture from us. They banned our language, dance, and even the giving of lei. Being brown was bad and surfing was evil. Worst of all, Hawaiians lost their land to the United States and an elite few.

For many, all that we had left was the sea. But even that was denied because foreigners claimed their land ownership extended into the ocean.

But this was changing because of the war and its aftermath. The great strike had cracked the monolith of power that controlled the islands. Returning servicemen were taking advantage of the G.I. Bill and getting a university and law school education. A storm was brewing, and I felt that *makani*, the wind, would sweep the islands and make changes for the better.

I watched the sea, loving its beauty. I rose as the band played Kalakaua's, *Hawai'i Pono 'i*, our national anthem. *Aloha aina, aloha kai,* filled my heart as I sang the words.

As my emotions rose I asked myself what I could do to save what I cared about. The great strike against the sugar plantations had opened the eyes of the workers that, united, they could control their lives and make it better.

Unfortunately, the Hawaiian was not getting a higher education. Is it because the missionaries had treated us as savages and lazy? Or because our monarchy had been stamped out by a few white men and Hawaiians did not resist the suppression that came afterwards? Despite being part of the United States, the racism of the Massie case showed that many people in America thought we were foul black people. The aftermath of the attack on Pearl Harbor demonstrated that Washington, D.C. believed that a large segment of the population of Hawai'i were disloyal to America. It took heroic efforts by young Japanese men to prove our government wrong.

I had just been with Uncle John, one of the original Beach Boys. Hawaiians and other locals like him practiced the surfing culture, played music and sang. They climbed coconut trees to get leaves to make hats, rings, and ornaments for the visitors. But is this the way to protect our land and the sea? Be thought of as the bronze man on the surfboard, the singer in a hotel, or the hula dancer in the Kodak picture show?

I realized that if I were to do anything of value I should get an education. It was a concept I resisted. It was easier to be a fisherman and live a stress-free life. But if I intended to participate in the sweeping changes coming to Hawai'i, I needed to change as well. Only in this way could I help protect our land and the sea.

CHAPTER 17

Boat Day

Matson's ship, the S.S. Lurline, was famous for its cruises to Hawai'i.
During the war years when it transported troops it was painted a dull gray.
Its return to the cruise business, repainted white, was a day of celebration.

President Harold W. Kent's announcement created excitement in the school. He said, "The Lurline is coming back to Hawai'i with visitors, and the men of Kamehameha will meet it."

Before the war, tourism had been a minor industry. Sugarcane, pineapple, and the military were the economy. But with the strike of 1946 and the continuing labor unrest, the agricultural base of Hawai'i was tottering. A return of visitors to the islands promised a source of revenue for the Big Five companies.

Assembled at the administration building, my classmates and I boarded buses for Waikiki. Once there, we dressed in *malos*, light brown cloths that wrapped around our waist and genitals. But unless you wound it carefully a danger existed that the skimpy outfit would unravel and leave you naked.

"Roy," I said. "How do you tie this thing? It keeps coming off."

"Not tight enough. I'll show you."

Roy grabbed the linen and wound it around my belly and completed the maneuver.

"Lucky I have washboard abs. Otherwise your tying would squeeze me to death."

"Come on, let's go."

We ran outside and helped manhandle outrigger canoes into the water. Girls from school offered lei. With my tight bindings, the cloying smell around my neck made me nauseous. I wanted to rid myself of the flowers, but we were warned, "Keep them on."

"Why?" I asked Gino who grasped an outrigger next to me as we pushed the vessel into the sea.

"All part of the act," Gino said. "We are the friendly natives wearing flowers and not carrying spears coming to meet the newcomers to the island."

"We are putting on a Hollywood show."

Gino shrugged, "If that's what the Colonel wants, that's what we do."

"I can't remember a time when the Lurine or Matsonia was met by canoes filled with natives."

"This event is special. It's the first Matson boat into the harbor with visitors since the war. Got to make it a big deal. If more tourists come, means money."

"So we are helping the Big Five."

"Yeah, but Uncle John is happy, maybe some lonely divorcee is sad, easy meat."

"I thought beach boys are not supposed to touch the tourists?"

"When you teach surfing, plenty touching. Woman want stand on the board, you got to hold them up."

"But what happens after? Hotel won't let a beach boy in."

"Tourist always forgets something. Uncle is just returning it to her room."

"That's the kind of life I want."

"You got to wait in line. Plenty want to be, but you must know someone."

We shoved the outrigger canoe into the ocean. It crested a wave, its pointed prow with the symbol of the war god rode high and then dipped down, smacking the water, showering me with water. It felt cool, but not cold. I wiped the salt away and hauled myself into the vessel along with the rest of our crew. There came a pause while other boats entered the water.

"Are you going to become a beach boy?" I asked.

"Yeah man, Uncle John will get me in," Gino answered.

"Why do it?"

"He calls it heaven. I want a taste of it."

We bobbed in the ocean waiting for the signal. Behind us, the sun started its rise above the mountains. Ahead, the horizon lost its grey as the light swept away the dark allowing the blue of morning to fill the sky. Low waves rolled in, less than two feet high, ripples on a mirror smooth surface.

"*Makaukau*, ready," came the command from the lead boat.

A hundred and forty boys raised their paddles.

"*Imua*, go forward," our leader yelled.

Into the water our blades plunged, the leaf shaped wood forced the many crafts through the sea. We headed for Honolulu Harbor. To get there we must go over the boiling surf at the edge of the fringing reef. Not an easy task, for if your canoe approaches broadside, the wave could push you over, and spill the crew into the sea.

Few of us were paddlers. My own experience had been in a tin canoe where the most important part of the venture is to stay afloat. That is hard to do in a can.

Our boat made it over the roiling waves. A few others went broadside into the surf, but none turned over. Our small flotilla assembled beyond the breakers and set out for the harbor.

I glimpsed the Lurline as it rounded Diamond Head, big, beautiful, and white. During the war, the navy had confiscated Matson's tourist ships. To avoid submarines, they had been camouflaged. After Japan surrendered, it took more than two years to get the ships ready for peacetime use.

As we paddled to stay ahead of the fast-approaching ship, I thought back to ancient times when Hawaiians had greeted Captain Cook and other foreigners. Hundreds of canoes filled with natives, food, and aloha welcomed them. But the friendly greetings were not always returned with kindness. Cook, angered by a theft, landed on shore with a party of marines and shot Hawaiians. Another foreign captain opened fire with his ship's cannon on canoes filled with men and women coming to greet him. It is said that three hundred died. Such massacres dampened the friendly attitude toward newcomers.

We passed Fort DeRussey, Kewalo Basin, and headed for the Aloha Tower. This ten story building, the tallest in all the islands, was built in 1926 to welcome tourists. On "Boat Day" before the war thousands came to see the tourist ship come in. Today there would be an extra special reception.

Slicing through the ocean, small waves ruffling the surface of the water at its prow, the Lurline entered the harbor. Its horn blew several blasts. From the shore there came a response. Our canoes raced ahead of the ship throwing flowers in its path. We yelled, "Aloha, aloha."

We drew back as the ship eased into the dock. A man raised his baton and swung it down and up in a decisive beat as the Royal Hawaiian Band played a rousing song. Once tied to the dock, a gangplank nuzzled up to the ship and visitors descended.

A glee club dressed in white with red sashes burst into a welcoming song. A half-dozen women in grass skirts with hollow brown coconuts covering their breasts began to swing and sway in a Hawaiian hula. Scores of other women with flower lei rushed to the arrivals, and draped their gifts around the necks of the visitors. More than a hundred thousand people came to greet seven hundred passengers.

With nothing better to do, I said to my friends, "Dive for coins."

In I went, waving my hand to those visitors still on board the ship. Pennies and nickels plunked into the water and twisted toward the bottom. I grabbed some and surfaced. Looking up I saw two Scotts wearing kilts.

"Do you think they have anything underneath those plaid tents?" I said.

"I don't know," Roy answered. "Let's swim closer and see."

We did and saw *olo'olo*.

"Go back," our leader ordered.

We returned to Waikiki. Pulling our canoe out of the water, I said to Roy, "I don't think I want to do this again, too much work and what do we get out of it?"

"Somebody is always using Kamehameha boys to play native. Before the war, the navy got a dozen students to go to Howland Island and live on it. The idea was to keep it away from the Japanese and British."

"Howland Island, isn't that where Amelia Earhart intended to land and refuel?"

"Right, our boys built a landing field for her. She never arrived."

"Why use Kamehameha students to occupy the island?"

"The place is flat and no food. The navy figured Hawaiian kids knew how to survive surrounded by sea."

"What happened when Pearl Harbor was attacked?"

"Howland Island was bombed by the Japanese. We lost some Kamehameha guys."

"Yeah, and the military grabbed ROTC students, gave them rifles and made them guard O'ahu beaches," Gino said.

"Until they found out that many were Japanese. Then they took away the guns and discharged them. Only Hawaiian boys were left to fight invaders. Our guys were unpaid and kept so long on guard duty that some of them never got their GED degree," Roy said.

"And then there is something like today, when browns are needed they call on Kamehameha," I said.

"But when we want jobs Big Five give us nothing. Go work in the fields or be a policeman," Roy complained.

"Or maybe like Gino, be a Beach Boy and entertain the tourists," I said.

"You're jealous," Gino answered giving me a punch on the arm.

We sparred for a bit until the student leader stopped us. We got to the lockers, changed, and headed out to the bus to return to school.

What my friends said troubled me. Hawaiians couldn't get good jobs. What use would college be if all you came back to is picking pineapple? I couldn't figure out how unions could help. All they did was strike and ask for more money.

When he was young, my father couldn't get a good job with the plantations and tried being a private businessman. He had many failures. Finally he borrowed from the bank to build his own theater, the Roxy. Everybody said, "At a thousand seats, the movie house is too big for Kaua'i." They appeared to be right when my dad faced foreclosure and bankruptcy. But war came. Soldiers garrisoned on Kaua'i. Needing entertainment, they came to our movie house and filled it continually.

Dad paid all his debts and made enough money to retire. He and mom lived in San Francisco. Once I got an education, I could take over the theater and run it for him. But the soldiers had left the island. We were back to pre-war days and dwindling show crowds.

Participating in "Boat Day" was a downer. My conversation with my friends made me realize that Hawaiians had no future in our homeland.

But where could I go? I had never been away from the security blanket of Hawai'i.

A joyous day for the Big Five proved depressing for me. I couldn't see how I could save the *aina,* the *kai,* or be successful.

CHAPTER 18

The Big Island of America

Statehood for Hawai'i became a heated topic for discussion in my political science class. "Resolved Hawai'i should be the 49th State. Anyone agree or disagree with this?" our teacher asked.

Being foolishly bold, I raised my hand and said, "We should be the next state because Hawai'i will finally have legislators who can vote. It will make a big difference since the islands would have two senators."

"Disagreement?" the teacher asked.

"Yeah, statehood is only good for the Big Five. There is nothing in it for Hawaiians," a student said.

"Moses, why do you say that?"

"My auntie told me, we lost the kingdom because the plantations wanted annexation to America to protect sugar sales. Hawaiians got nothing out of it. This is the same deal all over again."

"But isn't it a good idea to have votes in Congress like William said?"

Roy raised his hand, "But who will be elected? The Japanese, they vote in a bloc. Hawaiians would have no chance. Better a territory with an appointed governor."

Under the surface a racial pot was boiling. Since the coming of the missionaries, the islands had been dominated by a small group of conservative Republicans. They had protected their economic interests by keeping the races divided. Up until annexation there was no dominant ethnic group. But somehow the Japanese had kept coming to work in the sugar fields and now were almost forty percent of the population.

Distinguished service in the war had given the nisei a status that they had never enjoyed before. Plus, the returning soldiers were going to college and law school; from the mainland, union men were coming to educate the locals in how to seize power.

After class I asked Roy, "Do you believe if we get statehood the Japanese will take over?"

"That's what Senator Campbell says."

"But is that bad? If Japanese get elected fair and square isn't that okay? I have a Japanese uncle who served on the Kaua'i Board of Supervisors and he is a good guy."

Roy said nothing.

He made me think of our situation in Hawai'i. Political power is in the hands of the Big Five. So long as they are in control, the other races in the islands must get along with each other. They have to. Most people live at the subsistence level, sharing and helping each other is the only way to make it. But what if power could be seized by one ethnic group, would that create a division among the races?

Pan American Airways Stratocruiser Airplane
over San Francisco (Source: Wikipedia)

Summer vacation had arrived and a summons came to fly to California. The family would be taking a trip across the United States, into Canada as far as Quebec, head south into Mexico, and return through the southwest and Los Angeles to San Francisco.

A passport was not needed, but a birth certificate to prove you were a citizen and an ID card was necessary. I flew on a Boeing Pan American Stratocruiser, a premier airliner derived from the B-29 of World War II fame. It had four noisy radial engines and could make the trip from Hawai'i to San Francisco in ten hours.

It was a state of the art airship with sleeping berths for first class and a lower deck with a lounge and bar. Although I tried, I was turned away by a cute stewardess. Pan American knew how to pick them, slender, blonde, blue eyed, and single.

We left Honolulu with the sun blazing hot and arrived in darkness. Excitement gripped me as we landed at the city's airport. It wasn't much, a big tower, a debarkation building, and racks for unloaded baggage. I had scoffed at the idea of wearing a jacket. But once off the airplane the skin on my arms puckered, damp air filled my lungs, my body shivered in the light fog that hovered over the airfield. An aloha shirt did not protect you.

"Bags in the racks at the end of the terminal," a porter yelled.

"Immigration check," an officer said.

I reported to him but he sent me away to get my baggage.

Retrieving it I returned and waited in line. On my turn, the officer flipped open the locks and rummaged through my clothes as if the crown jewels of India were hidden in my bag.

"Got a passport," he said.

"No, birth certificate," I said.

"Let's see it and some ID."

Scrutinizing my documents he said, "You're a Mexican."

"No, Portuguese-Hawaiian."

"Look Mexican to me."

"My birth certificate shows I was born in the Territory of Hawai'i."

"You look like a Spic to me."

"Whatever that is, I'm not."

The officer gave me a rude look and said, "Get out of here."

Walking away, my legs wobbled, my heart thumped. This is a new experience. I noticed that brown and Asian passengers were targeted by the immigration man, all others walked out with just a nod. Shaken by the experience it took me a little time to remember the instructions I had received by letter, "Catch the airport bus and we'll meet you at the terminal."

It was an amazing ride. The highway led to a lighted metropolis with buildings taller than the Aloha tower. In the night, San Francisco looked like Oz's Emerald City. Street lights, traffic signals, honking autos were everywhere. This is not Kaua'i where there isn't a stop sign on the island.

In the bus station hundreds of people milled around like buzzing bees. There weren't any flower lei only scarves around the neck and warm coats. I shivered as I left the bus, realizing that I am not as tough as I thought. The old adage, "When in Rome do as the Romans do" popped into my head. Short-sleeved aloha shirts are okay in Hawai'i, but not in San Francisco.

Mom and cousin Pono met me, bundled me onto a bus, and we headed up Market Street. I gasped for this was the widest road I had ever seen. Stopping at a street light, a shrill clanging drew me to a red and yellow trolley crossing the street, its iron wheels grinding on the rails that threaded up a hill. Far away, a mournful sound hooted, warning others of a ship's passage in the bay.

We got off the bus at Central Avenue and walked to 158, a three story San Francisco Victorian. "Wow, is this home?" I said.

"Our house," Mom answered.

The resentment I felt for being abandoned for years, washed away. A sense of pride came over me as I realized that a once illiterate cowboy and a dirt poor cannery worker earning four cents a day had achieved success in life.

With minimal schooling, at eight years old, my dad went to work on the Parker Ranch in Hawai'i. He ran away from the Big Island to make a better life for himself in Honolulu. He tried many vocations, had several failures, and finally settled on showing movies. Mom and dad built the thousand seat Roxy Theater, and the war made them a fortune. Retired to San Francisco, he and mom returned to school for an education. Two landless Hawaiians had beaten the odds and become successful.

The next few days were absorbed in preparations for our trip and waiting for my sister to finish college. I rode buses, visited stores, walked the streets and decided that San Francisco is a beautiful city. My opinion was reinforced by Herb Caen, a columnist who called the city "Baghdad by the Bay".

Everyone looked pale. Maybe it was a lack of sunshine. I noticed people giving me a second glance. My father answered my concern saying, "You are as black as the ace of spades."

I thought about the Massie case and the navy's hatred of blacks. Was this true in San Francisco? I couldn't wash my color away. What would it be like when we got on the road?

"We are leaving," my mother said, rousting me out of bed. Dressed, the family headed for the Greyhound bus station and started our trip across America. California is vast and especially interesting as you ride up into the

Sierra Mountains. At Truckee for a rest stop, I heard about the Donner party. At the cash register I asked the woman attendant what happened.

"Long time ago a bunch of people from back east tried to make it through Donner Pass in winter time. They got snowed in. Starved, they ate each other to survive. Come spring, only half of them were still alive."

"It sounds ugly, people eating each other."

"Yes, that's why the story is famous, cannibalism."

I got on the bus and the driver announced, "Next stop Reno, Nevada, the biggest little city in the world."

I said to my sister, "How can you be the biggest and the littlest?"

"It's advertising," Colleen answered.

My sister is a pretty woman, slender, with a figure like a model. She has delicate hands, maybe because of her piano playing. She is intelligent with a stubborn streak. Because of this and being four years older we always got into fights. But on this trip we decided to work together to make it through whatever adventures we would have.

Driving into Reno, there is a sign that announces: RENO BIGGEST LITTLE CITY IN THE WORLD. By San Francisco standards it's not big, but it's noisy. Arcade lights, flashing signs, whirring slot machines, whoops and hollers as money poured out of them. The bus came to a stop and we got off heading for our hotel.

Unpacking, I said, "Let's see the town."

"You can't gamble," Mom said.

"Don't go near where there's drinking," Dad ordered.

With my sister in tow, I scooted downstairs. Blue sky canopied above us. Clouds were absent. Darkness shrouded the mountains, their jagged peaks outlined by snow. Cold wind stung my face. My cheeks tingled. With this severe cold in June, I understood how the Donner pioneers didn't make it over the mountains in winter.

Lawyer signs plastered several buildings. One of them said: "Divorce Capitol of the World". I spied an open cigar store near a bridge spanning the Truckee River. "Let's find out about this divorce stuff."

"Don't go," my sister said. "Father doesn't want us near smoking."

I scooted in and saw a bearded man behind a counter.

"Hi mister," I said. "Why is Reno called the 'Divorce Capitol'?

"Where are you from?"

"Hawai'i."

"Most states and your place too only allow divorces for adultery."

"What's that?"

"When a married person makes love to another. In Reno you can get a divorce for any old reason. That building over there is the courthouse and you see that bridge by my shop, when the judge grants a divorce, the woman comes to that bridge and throws her wedding ring into it."

I ran out and said, "There's a lot of diamonds in that river. Let's go fishing."

"Water's too cold. You'll freeze to death," Colleen answered.

I searched the Truckee for a glint of jewels and saw nothing. Reluctantly, I gave up. We walked back to the hotel. Gamers hollered. Stacks of big silver dollars were everywhere. I wondered how to get some. Dice rolled on a green table with numbers. I heard the words, "Lucky seven. Oh hell, craps."

I flashed back to the side door at the Roxy Theater where GIs rolled dice against the wall. They whooped or moaned depending on what the numbered cubes showed when they stopped rolling.

We left Reno early in the morning for Salt Lake City. Nevada is dry, featureless, and flat. Our bus rolled up a low hill and down a sloping road and then up another slight hill and down again. We drove hundreds of miles up and down.

I was excited to see the Mormon city. Before the war the movie *Brigham Young* had played at the Roxy. Dynamic Dean Jagger had acted as the church's leader. He fought persecution in Illinois, escaped from death, and led his believers to Utah and founded Salt Lake City in 1847.

What fascinated me about the Mormon story was the coming of nine missionaries to Hawai'i three years later. They founded the Church of Latter-Day Saints and told of a revelation from God that the Hawaiians are one of the twelve lost tribes of Israel.

When I heard of it, the claim blew my mind for scientists said the Polynesians started their Pacific journeys from China. If the vision the Mormons have is right, it appeared the archeologists are wrong. We came from Mesopotamia via the Persian Gulf, traveled east along a chain of islands, and finally settled in Hawai'i.

A boring ride gave way to anticipation as we entered Utah. Once in Salt Lake City I thought I would find real evidence of the 'Lost Tribe' claim.

Learn about the sea gulls. Test the buoyancy of the lake. Find out about Gabriel on the top of the Tabernacle.

Arrival in the city was uneventful. After we settled in the hotel, Dad announced, "Up early in the morning for the tour."

At dawn we entered the tourist bus and headed out. Salt Lake City is the cleanest metropolis I had ever seen. Its air smelled sweet. The streets are wide. Houses and buildings are relatively low to the ground compared to San Francisco. But that is understandable since the city is not built on hills.

The tourist guide kept up a running chatter. As we passed the Tabernacle she said, "You see that angel on top of it? Anyone know who it is?"

My hand shot up. "Gabriel," I said.

"Wrong. Gabriel is on Mont St. Michel in France. That angel is the Mormon hero Moroni and do you know what he is trumpeting?"

The bus was silent especially since I sat on my hands and didn't want to make a fool of myself.

"He is announcing to the world that the fullness of the Gospel of Jesus Christ has been restored to the earth."

"What does she mean?" I asked Colleen.

"I don't know."

"We are passing the Great Salt Lake. Brigham Young founded this city on its shores when he arrived from Illinois. The water is buoyant. You cannot sink and will float on top like a cork. At one time the lake covered all of Utah, parts of Nevada, and Idaho. Fish cannot survive in the salty water. But it is claimed that a monster, part crocodile with the head of a horse, lives in it."

This far-fetched story got my interest. It went along with the legend of the miracle of the seagulls depicted in *Brigham Young*.

Right on cue, the guide announced, "We will stop at the seagull monument and tell you what happened a hundred years ago."

We left the bus and stared at a tower, with a figure of a white bird on top. The guide began her story, "After Brigham Young arrived, the settlers planted crops to avoid starvation. Once the plants grew, the people prepared for an abundant harvest, but millions of crickets came eating everything."

I remembered the movie; Jagger, Tyrone Power, and Linda Darnell beating with brooms, shovels, anything that was flat to kill the insects. But the hordes kept coming. The tension of the actors on the silver screen grew as the fight against the swarms appeared hopeless. The Mormons would starve.

"But then the miracle came," the tour guide said, ending my daydream. "Sea gulls from the lake and the surrounding waterways came and ate the critters. They filled up their stomachs, went to the lake, vomited, and came back to eat some more. The gulls saved the settlers."

I wanted to clap, like I did at the end of the movie, but restrained myself. Some people scoff at miracles, the monument is proof that they happen.

Then our bus motored to Heritage Park, climbed a hill, and stopped at a long rectangular structure. "This Is The Place Monument," our guide said. "It was dedicated last year to mark the Centennial celebration of the founding of Salt Lake City. After fifteen hundred miles of trekking, those are the words Brigham Young uttered when he arrived on top of Pioneer View one hundred and one years ago."

We left the bus following our guide. A bronze placard attached to the stone read: Brigham Young July 24, 1847. Above it stood a statue looking west. Along the sides of the monument were other figures of metal in pioneer garb.

"Joseph Smith, founder of the Mormon faith, was assassinated for his religious beliefs. The rest of his followers led by Young fled, following a trail blazed by the Donner party. They wanted to live free and practice their religion," our guide said.

As she spoke, I relived the movie. A dream came to Young of a 'Promised Land.' He gathered his believers and they set out traveling over an unforgiving landscape and a path plagued by Indians. After many miles they came to this hill and saw a wide valley and a lake. Their perilous journey was over, but their troubles were just beginning.

"Plymouth Rock is an emblem of people escaping persecution for their beliefs and creating this nation. This monument is a marker commemorating the men and women who subdued this country from the Missouri River to the Pacific Ocean," our guide said.

The woman's words and my remembrances of the movie made me realize that for years, people of different persuasions from the majority had fled from bigotry and hatred to find a land where they could live in freedom. I thought of Hawai'i and the movement of Polynesians from one island to another as they sought freedom from the tyranny of their homeland. But in today's world there is no place to escape to.

We left Salt Lake City heading for Chicago. I was impressed by what a few pioneers, seeking to worship God in their own way, had been able to accomplish. They had built a beautiful city and great state.

The further we traveled the more I realized there aren't any areas of the world you could run to in order to escape intolerance and racial oppression. Somehow you had to deal with it where you lived or remain suppressed.

CHAPTER 19

Growing Knowledge

After a long journey through Idaho, Wyoming, and Nebraska, we arrived in Saint Louis, Missouri. The city was named after a French king. At one time a huge part of America was owned by France. Napoleon Bonaparte, engaged in European war, offered his nation's property to Thomas Jefferson. Even though the Constitution did not authorize the acquisition of territory, the President bought the land for fifteen million dollars.

I mention this stop not because of the wonders of the former French city, but my jolting experience with meeting a person of the Jewish faith. Growing up on Kaua'i, I had not been aware of a religion known as Judaism. I did not realize that there was a deadly stigmata attached to a person wearing the Star of David until after World War II and the revelations of the Holocaust and the Nazi death camps.

My parents had done a good job of planning our continental tour. With the help of AAA, they had mapped out every stop and arranged for hotels in advance. After the bus let us off, we taxied to our hotel. Although the hotel clerk gave us suspicious looks and asked many questions, he allowed us to check in. I was uneasy about the man's inquiries. I thought he didn't like people of color or our last name.

Famished, I got permission to go downstairs. On a stand by the clerk's desk, a newspaper headline said: "**RUSSIANS BLOCKADE BERLIN**". Pausing to read the article, I noticed a pudgy man with a woman behind him entering through the gold bordered glass doors. Both were richly dressed and the lady sported diamond rings on her fingers and bracelets encrusted with jewels.

Perspiration beaded the man's head as he came to the front desk and said, "We would like a room for the night."

"Do you have a reservation?" The clerk asked.

"No."

"Let me see what I have. Would you sign the register please with your address?"

The man did so. I thought it a little strange he did not ask about cost.

"Aha," the clerk said, "we have this very nice suite…."

He stopped speaking, his eyes widened as he looked at the page in the hotel book. "Finkelstein! You're Jewish."

"Yes."

"We don't accept your kind in this hotel or colored people."

"But, I have money. I can pay what you ask."

"You are not wanted here. Leave." The hotel keeper said rudely.

"Is there any hotel in this town that accepts Jews? This is the third one we have tried."

"I will not help you. Just go," the clerk said as if the man and his wife had a dreadful disease.

The Jewish people turned away, speaking in a language I couldn't understand. A porter, who had brought in two valises, laid them on the hotel floor and walked away. The couple picked them up and stepped through the gold glass doors.

What is this? I thought. Jews and people of color are not permitted in a public hotel? I wondered why the clerk had paused when he saw my father's name. "Fernandez," he said. "Spanish?"

"Portuguese," Dad answered.

The clerk nodded as if we had passed a smell test. The way he spoke to the Jewish man made me wonder if he had an offensive odor.

I guess Portuguese people are considered Caucasian. But we are Hawaiian too. Would that have made a difference? On the mainland my mom always talked about being French. She probably would fit right into Saint Louis, founded by French fur trappers. My sister is pale and passes for white. My dark color was fading and the European half of my being taking hold. But the further we traveled, what prejudice would we meet?

I may be naïve. The people on isolated Kaua'i are mostly Asian, Filipinos, and Portuguese. In Honolulu my first inkling of racial bias came from the battles between the military and locals. From what I had learned from the Massie case, the white military considered us blacks and dealt with Hawaiians as they did with the former American slaves.

What was wrong with being Jewish? I didn't dare ask the clerk for he stood at his desk shaking in anger. Should I go outside and speak with the two people? But how do you ask strangers, "Why don't people like you?" What terrible things, if any, had they done to cause Hitler to exterminate them? There is a barrier being dark. I had just learned there is a barrier to being white and Jewish.

After dad and I went to bed we were awakened by a man running down the hall yelling, "Fire, fire."

Alarmed, we dressed, left our other clothes, and evacuated the third floor room via the stairs to the street. I noticed a naked man as white as new snow. A soldier, he had fallen asleep in his room with a lighted cigarette and set his mattress on fire.

Once the blaze was extinguished we were allowed upstairs. M.P.s came to gather up the soldier. Since we were the same size, they asked if I would lend him clothes. I did.

Watching him dress, I could see no difference between him and me except for my brown skin. This trip was giving me a new view of the world. Was it safer to live in Hawai'i and never go beyond its shores?

We headed for Chicago, called the "Windy City" for the fierce winds that blew out of the Great Lakes. In the winter time it froze anyone who dared to go out. The name is a French word for the Indian phrase: Stinky Onion.

As usual, my knowledge of the city was based on what I learned from the movies: Scarface, Al Capone, Lucky Luciano, Saint Valentine's Day massacre, Tommy guns, illegal booze, easy women, and corrupt cops and politicians.

I didn't learn anything about gangsters. What I did see was a horrid elevated rail system. The iron cars rattled by our hotel room, the wheels screeching like mynah birds having a fight. When the train started up I felt trembling in our room like the rumbles of a Kilauea earthquake.

While touring the city, I learned of Mrs. O'Leary milking a cow that kicked over a kerosene lantern setting her barn ablaze and causing the "Great Chicago Fire". This was like my hometown, Kapa'a, where a kerosene lantern in a garage set the town on fire, destroying half of it.

From what I learned, it might not have been Mrs. O'Leary's fault but some news reporter making up a story. Because of the Potato Famine, starving, poor Irish left the Emerald Island and settled in America. Their immigration created a huge wave of anti-Irish sentiment along the east coast. This animosity spread west. It was not uncommon to blame the Irish for a catastrophe.

We left for Detroit and excitement, a new car. For years we had driven trucks. It is a useful vehicle. But to take families on trips it is not the best.

At the Buick factory, dad drove out with a black four door limousine. A grand car, the most beautiful we ever owned. It drove like a dream, all the way into Canada, past Montreal, and onward to Quebec.

The city is old Europe, with cobbled streets, brick buildings, and walls to guard against attackers. Once settled in our hotel, which was cool despite it being mid-summer, we joined a guided tour. Our leader, Nicole had dark hair and eyes, a narrow face and a prominent nose. In a shrill voice she said, "French explorers were the first to colonize Canada which means New France. Quebec became the first permanent city of the colony. It grew larger as fur trading increased."

In boring detail she described the city's growth pointing out several old buildings constructed in the 18th century. My hearing perked up when she said, "The rapid growth of British colonies to the south made it inevitable that war would come."

Nicole launched into the famous story of the British General, Wolfe, making a surprise attack early in the morning. "But as the enemy climbed the steep hill that you see, French geese honked awakening Marquis de Montcalm and his soldiers. A battle was fought. Both leaders were killed and Canada became a colony of Britain.

"But we remain French to this day." She finished the history lesson and kept us moving along the streets pointing out historical buildings and places. I sensed that there was more to the story then she had related. When I had the opportunity I said, "*Madame, j'ai suis Francais*," in my best high school French.

"*Comment?*"

"*Mon Grand Pere citoyen du Alsace-Lorraine.*"

"*Vous ete American.*"

"*Oui mais Francais aussi.*"

"*D'accord.*" Then Nicole rattled off sentences in French.

I said, "My French is weak. Can we speak in English?"

She nodded.

"You said that Quebec continues to be French, but aren't you governed by the British?"

"That is true, but we are a minority and badly treated. My people want to be separated from the rest of Canada, form our own nation, under the protection of France."

"Is religion a factor? I see many Catholic churches in this city."

"Yes, religion is a part of the reason for separation. But it is also the preservation of our French culture. We need to have sovereignty to keep our heritage and faith in God."

Our conversation ended leaving me much to ponder. The French were like the Hawaiians, conquered people who feared losing what was dear to them, their culture.

We left the city and I said to my sister, "I feel kindred to the people of Quebec."

"Yes, I do too. The churches are the same as ours and the people whom I met were very nice."

"Good Catholics," Mom said.

We drove in silence into Maine. We spent the night by a lake and next day traveled south through New England heading for Boston. The scenery was beautiful. The towns well laid out. Buildings and homes maintained to perfection with trees everywhere, and not a skyscraper to be seen.

Boston had the old world flavor of Quebec, cobbled streets and red brick buildings. Most important were the museums and historical sites.

"Taxation without representation," had been the early cry of Bostonians as they heaved the king's tea into Boston harbor. George the Third responded by sending troops. Massacre followed. Patrick Henry sounded the cry for revolution, "I know not what others may do, but as for me give me liberty or give me death."

The general in Boston made the fatal mistake of marching north on Lexington to seize armament stockpiles and revolutionary leaders. Paul Revere made his famous ride to warn the countryside yelling, "The British are coming. The British are coming."

Columns of redcoats marched into Lexington. On the commons, the king's men fired on Americans, killing several. They did not fire back. People in the colonies hesitated breaking with England.

The soldiers marched north, and at a bridge on the edge of Lexington, they fired on masses of minutemen mustered across the river. The colonists fired back. It was "the shot heard round the world." The American Revolution was on.

"The British got a whipping from the Americans as they fled back to Boston," I said to Colleen as we stood on the bottom of Bunker Hill.

My five-foot-two-inch mom came up to us, her face wreathed in a smile. "I'm glad we came here, "she said, "I always wanted to learn about independence. You are the history boy. When you get home, you can tell everybody all about it."

Bill aboard the U.S.S. Constitution ("Old Ironsides")
in Boston Harbor. In the War of 1812 it defeated British ships.

Dad walked slowly from the tour bus. He was sixty-eight, seventeen years older than mother. Like most men of his age he had a large pot belly that dripped over his belt line. This overflow of stomach was not evident because my father always dressed well, wearing a coat and tie. It was not unusual for travelers post-war to look sharp with men wearing suits and women in nice dresses. Only a kid could get by with a pair of clean pants and a short-sleeved white shirt.

A dark grey hat covered dad's bald head. When doing business he wore a black toupee, which was somewhat noticeable for his side hair was dead white. To keep up the illusion that he was younger than his age, he shaved every day for if he failed to do so, the resulting beard would be white. Admittedly there was a certain amount of vanity in our dressing well, but pop did not want any of us to look shabby as we went through a land of people we did not know.

"A tough walk coming up the hill," Dad said, a wheeze evident in his voice.

"Yes, but it's worth it," Colleen answered. "There is a great view of Boston and the harbor."

"That's why the Americans occupied this spot. So that they could place cannon on it and shoot at the English ships," I said, reading from a guide book. "The British had to get rid of them before they could do damage. Up the hill they charged.

The rebel commander said, 'Don't shoot until you see the whites of their eyes.' Deadly was the fire when it came. It took three attacks to get rid of the Americans. They only left the hill because they were out of ammunition."

"You're better than the guide," Mom said.

"I'm excited to be here," I answered. "This is the place our country got started and because of what those early people did, I am proud to be an American."

We left Boston with mixed feelings. On the one hand, the fight for freedom proved wonderful to learn about, but the intolerance displayed by events like the Salem witch trials and the eradication of Indian tribes along the east coast were unfortunate results of the growth of a new nation. By seeing the environment that the New England missionaries grew up in, I understood how they could be strict and uncompromising when they came to Hawai'i to "convert the heathen."

CHAPTER 20

New York and Washington D.C.

My vision of New York was of a giant ape on top of the Empire State building, swatting bi-planes. King Kong's fight to save the love of his life imprinted on my mind from the first day it played at my father's movie theater. Today I would visit the tallest building in the world to see the site of that epic battle.

Leaving our hotel, I paused to read the newspaper. All land and water access to the former German capitol had been blocked by the Soviet Union. There were only three twenty-mile air corridors into the city. Hundreds of allied aircraft attempted to keep Berlin alive by transporting goods to it.

Speculation ran high that we were on the brink of World War Three. America had the threat of the atomic bomb but the Russians fielded a huge army of troops and tanks. This overwhelming ground force could pulverize all the Western European nations up to the English Channel. Would President Truman use our super weapon against white people as he did against the Japanese?

Considering the brinksmanship occurring between the two great powers, there was a genuine concern that war could break out at any moment.

Despite this fear, the news media wrote that you should not appease Stalin like Chamberlin appeased Hitler at Munich ten years ago.

I expressed my worry to dad as the elevator whizzed the family to the observation deck on top of the tallest building in the world. "Is war coming?"

My father stood silent.

I turned to my sister. She and mom chatted about shopping. If they weren't worried, why should I?

The elevator reached the top. I headed out into a gale of wind. New York City spread out before me. How Kong climbed to the top with Fay Wray then fought airplanes with one hand could only happen in Hollywood.

We toured other sights and in the afternoon Dad said, "We are going to visit with some of the boys from the "Fighting Sixty Ninth.""

These were service men that had come from New York to defend Kaua'i.

When we met them at a Bronx restaurant, we had tears in our eyes as we hugged. Inside there was talk of the early days of the war. We spoke of friends killed in action and received overwhelming thanks for treating lonely soldiers with warm aloha. What a contrast between Kaua'i and Honolulu with its "rap the haole syndrome".

Stanley, Andy, and their wives took us everywhere, Coney Island, the Great White Way, Central Park, and a Broadway show. Visiting the weathered-green Statue of Liberty, I found a brass plaque inside the pedestal supporting the one-hundred and fifty foot symbol. It read in part, "Give me your tired, your poor, your humbled masses yearning to be free…"

"These are great words," I said to Andy.

"Yeah, it's okay, but when my father came he had to live in Little Italy. The Jews had their ghettos and the Irish the same. We didn't mix like I saw in Hawai'i."

"What about the colored people?"

"They didn't live near us. Up in Harlem. Northern part of the city."

"Black people didn't soldier with you guys?"

"Military didn't mix coloreds with whites. Too many fights."

We fell silent.

I thought of the words on the plaque. How stirring they were, but living in America didn't ensure freedom from discrimination. How had the twenty-two ethnic groups brought to Hawai'i to work in the sugar fields escaped intolerance and battles between races?

Fighting 69th soldiers
Stanley on left, Andy on right

We left New York with warm feelings about our friends from the "Fighting 69th". Traveling past Philadelphia I wanted to make a side trip to Gettysburg, but the answer was no.

"If we don't get to Washington before dark we could lose our hotel reservation," Dad explained. Traveling in post-war America is not like it is today, where a credit card will hold a room. Back then reservations expired if not claimed in a timely fashion.

Washington, D.C., is different from Boston with its red brick buildings and New York with its skyscrapers. The avenues are broad, paved, and without bricks cobbled together. Government buildings are white, imposing, but not towering.

On the tour bus the next day, our guide said, "The District of Columbia is not a state. It is under the exclusive control of Congress. We will make our first stop at the Smithsonian Museum. It is named for a British Scientist, James Smithson, who willed his fortune to America for an 'institution of knowledge.'"

I wanted to see the airplane that Lindbergh flew across the Atlantic. I searched for it and found it hanging in a gallery, the words "Spirit of Saint Louis" stenciled on the metal behind the propeller. My sister dragged me away from the airship saying, "Let's find the Hope Diamond. It is cursed."

For some reason, I thought of Sherlock Holmes and the *Sign of the Four*. It is a story of India, hidden treasure, and death. The grand blue stone we looked for originated in India.

"This institution is called, 'America's attic'. Millions of items are donated every year, too many to be put on display. Please everyone, on the bus," our guide said.

We drove toward the Potomac River. "Look at the cherry trees. It's too bad it is not springtime when they blossom. They are beautiful then," Colleen said.

"The plants came from Japan," our guide said as we left the bus. "They are called *sakura*."

"You find a picture of it on the Japanese playing cards," mother added.

"I remember it. Big points if you get that card," I said.

The guide interrupted our conversation saying, "This is the Lincoln Memorial. Follow the line of the Reflecting Pond and you will see the Washington Monument, that structure is the tallest obelisk in the world, five-hundred-and-fifty-five feet. It is dedicated to President George Washington, a man called by his peers, "First in war, first in peace, and first in the hearts of his countrymen".

"Washington's monument was finished in 1885, eighty-six years after our first president's death. Lincoln died in 1865 and his memorial was dedicated in 1922. You can see that although these were great men and we owe them much, it can take a long time before the government will spend the money to honor them. Unlike the simple pointed structure beyond the reflecting pool, Lincoln's building is in the style of a Greek Doric Temple. It has thirty six columns representing the states at the time of the President's assassination."

Our guide invited us to tour the building. A nineteen foot tall statue of Lincoln sits in the back-middle of the structure. His head is slightly bent and he gazes with sad eyes right at you. On the walls are chiseled in stone two of his great speeches.

I read the first part of his Gettysburg address. "Four score and seven years ago our forefathers brought forth upon this continent a new nation, conceived in liberty, and dedicated to the proposition that all men are created equal…" Equality, that is the key word, I thought. All people are equal no matter their color, race, religion, or sex.

Despite Lincoln's broad vision of our "new nation,'" from the evidence on our trip I realized his "equal treatment for all" concept had not been achieved in America. I worried as I thought of driving into the "deep south". From the Massie trial, I knew that southern folk believed the murder of a Hawaiian is justified for an alleged rape of a white woman. "I'm from the south and we have a way of dealing with *niggers*," Grace Fortescue, mother of Theola Massie, said before her trial for manslaughter.

From what occurred in Hawai'i many years ago, it was clear to me that in the Civil War south, the slightest offense by a brown or black against white folk, whether real or imagined, would result in a lynching. For those interested in the case, the Pinkerton investigation after the trials came to the conclusion that Theola Massie had never been raped. The five local boys accused of the crime were innocent.

We left Washington for Knoxville, Tennessee. My heart beat faster. My face and hands were still brown.

My father is accustomed to perilous traveling. As a mail carrier, he had braved the wild countryside of the Parker Ranch on Hawai'i Island. During the counter-revolution against the Republic of Hawai'i he served as a mounted policeman in Honolulu. Showing motion pictures throughout the Orient, he toured the Philippines shortly after the insurgency against America was quelled. He loved to travel and visit interesting places and meet new people. From his bravery I took courage as we plunged headlong into the heart of Civil War America to visit my cousin, Arthur Morgan.

CHAPTER 21

Southern Experiences

"Created by Congress in 1933 to control flooding and provide electric power to the Tennessee Valley, the Tennesee Valley Authority is the largest producer of electricity in the United States," Cousin Arthur said on a tour of a dam overlooking a lake of water.

"Another one of Roosevelt's WPA projects," my Republican father said.

"The TVA is something different. Private companies controlled electric power generation before the depression. Roosevelt wanted to break that monopoly and have the federal government take control of power resources. He chose the Tennessee Valley to make a start since the farmland was not productive and families were living on a hundred dollars a year."

"I'm happy you have a good job, but this is just another example of government interfering with private enterprise."

"It needed to be done. Companies along the valley couldn't supply enough power. Flooding ruined farmland. This government enterprise saved Tennessee. People love the TVA."

"I need to go to the bathroom," I said.

Arthur gestured towards a building. I walked to it and saw a dingy door with a big sign "Blacks"

To the right I saw another sign saying, "Whites."

I looked at my arms. Where to go? I heard footsteps behind me. A black man walked by striding into the bathroom for colored folk. Comparing his skin to mine, I realized I am not dark. With my heart in my throat, I stumbled to the other toilet.

Inside, a man stood at a stall. He eyed me for a moment and looked away. I passed the sight test, but as I walked to an open urinal I wondered if I would pass the smell test. Blacks, I had been told when I entered Tennessee, had a terrible odor.

I heard a toilet flush and the man walked toward me. Maybe I imagined this, but I thought he sniffed the air several times. Tension rose as the footsteps slowed. Expecting to hear dreadful words I rushed my performance and headed out.

A drinking fountain stood anchored near the door, a sign above it read, "Whites Only."

Should I chance it? The man would be coming out soon.

Before this trip, the movies had provided my only knowledge of America. From the manager of the Lihu'e Theater on Kaua'i, I learned of what he called the greatest movie ever made, *Birth of a Nation*. "I've seen it sixty-eight times," he said. He recounted how white-sheeted men of the Ku Klux Klan eliminated the black threat to the white race.

As I stood near the water cabinet I imagined a flaming cross erected in a field with figures staring through holes poked through hoods ready to accomplish my lynching. The door next to me creaked open. I sucked in air, went to the fountain, drank, washed my hands, and watched the white gentleman leave.

"Darn," I said. "The Massie case has spooked me."

Slightly shaken, I returned to the family and we left for Arthur's home. His honey blond wife with bright blue eyes met us at the door. Slender, with her hair coiffed short and wrapped closely around her head like a Roman helmet, Gladys welcomed us with a charm that she described as southern hospitality. When we told her that we planned to visit Atlanta, Georgia, she said, "You must meet my parents."

I will skip details of our Tennessee visit and hasten to Atlanta. Gladys accompanied us on our drive. The city is picturesque, but I remembered little of it. I did ask my cousin's wife about the fire that I witnessed in "Gone with the Wind."

"Everything has been rebuilt. But people have not forgiven Sherman for what he did."

We traveled beyond Atlanta into farm country where fields of low shrubs grew. There were thousands of white balls, like frozen puffs of smoke, nestled among the leaves.

We came to a southern home and were welcomed with a civility that reminded me of the opening scenes of *"Gone with the Wind."* A barbecued chicken dinner followed by a visit on a spacious green lawn, made our family believe we were treasured friends.

As day turned into night, I saw lights flitting near me.

"Fireflies," Gladys said.

I chased them. Watching the glow of the insects die and spring up again, I captured one to learn its secret. But I feared my clumsiness might cause its death, and let it go. I returned to my chair and drank a mint julep. Everything around me stood calm and peaceful. The conversation droned on and I fell asleep.

We left the next day for New Orleans. It is a long drive and I spelled my dad at the wheel. My imagination ran wild as I thought of the Pirate Jean Lafitte, the French Quarter, and Mardi Gras. The thought of Creole cooking and Louisiana shrimps made my stomach rumble with anticipation.

I was unprepared for the segregation in Louisiana. Restaurants would not serve blacks. As I walked on the sidewalk I noticed colored people jumping into the gutter to avoid confrontations with white men. At open-air lunch counters along the streets there weren't any people of color being served. I wondered if I would be allowed to buy something to eat, but decided not to test the temper of the local people.

When I rode on a bus the black folks always moved to the rear. I usually took a middle position even if I had to stand.

Politeness marked my experiences with people of color. They said, "Yes, sir or no, sir" and nothing more. I didn't see many of them for they lived their lives in segregated neighborhoods.

Dad and Mom decided to cut our visit to New Orleans short. He had stopped there primarily to get money wired to him from Hawai'i. We left for Texas, the Alamo, and more discrimination.

In San Antonio we met our first taste of hatred against Hispanics. Mexicans were not allowed to register in the hotel my family had chosen. It took a lot of talking to convince the clerk to accept us as Portuguese-Hawaiians. The man made a snide remark, "We don't want any Zoot Suiters here."

His comment resonated with me. The Damon Tract riots in 1945, where American service men beat up locals in that housing area who they called "Zoot Suiters". This mirrored other attacks in Los Angeles and Texas between sailors, marines, and young Hispanics who wore Zoot Suits. These are black woolen suits with broad shoulders tapering down to narrow trouser legs and a long chain hanging down. The riots in Los Angeles started the same way as the riots in Honolulu, servicemen harassing brown women and local men retaliating.

As usual, we took a tour. Our group leader gave us background history leading up to the battle of the Alamo. "Texas belonged to Spain. Revolutionaries in Mexico declared independence from that country and the Spanish province of Texas became part of their new nation. American settlers established themselves in this territory and trouble started between the colonists and Mexico over taxes and slavery. Sam Houston led the Americans in a war of independence. President General Santa Ana brought a Mexican army north to destroy the revolutionaries. While Houston gathered his forces, a small group of Texans reinforced this old Spanish mission called "The Alamo".

I listened to the guide recounting the thirteen day battle and the massacre of the two hundred defenders including Davy Crockett and Jim Bowie. He finished saying, "The ferocious killing of all the Alamo defenders enraged the colonists. Sam Houston's forces defeated Santa Ana's army a month later, and established the Republic of Texas which soon became part of the United States."

From comments I heard around me, I realized that hostility towards Mexican people continued a hundred years after Texas became a state. Signs on restaurants said: "We Serve Whites Only No Spanish or Mexicans".

Upsetting to me was the story of half-a-million Mexicans being deported "south of the border". Among them were American citizens. This rejection of brown people occurred during the Great Depression. It was evident to me that in times of great stress our country can be cruel to its citizens of color.

My father interrupted my miserable thoughts and delivered the *coup de gras*, "We are driving into Mexico to see Monterrey."

"Dad, they might not let us back in," I said.

"I want to see Mexico," my sister answered.

I knew her vote was decisive. But what did she have to worry about? She could pass for the Disney character, Snow White.

Out-voted, I sat glumly in the Buick as we went through the American border check. I imagined that the police men were happy to see Hispanics going home. I suspected the trouble would come when we tried to get back in.

It came as a surprise when the Mexican side proved worse. An officer in white with medals on his uniform, a red sash across his chest, and a rattling saber at his side poked through our suitcases as if we were bringing dangerous substances into Mexico. While he skewered our clothes with his sword, his minions examined every inch of the car, even removing seats.

As the search continued, the pompous man called the general said, "Mr. Fernandez, you say that you're not Mexican."

"Portuguese-Hawaiian," my father answered, a genial tone in his voice.

"Oh, you are Hawaiian, come into my office."

Dad returned after several minutes, and said, "We can go."

Minions put seats and luggage back into the car and we drove off.

"Bill, what happened?" Mom said.

"He wanted money. He called it an entry tax. I gave him twenty dollars."

Monterrey was founded in the 16th century. Under Spanish rule it remained a small village. It grew to city size when Mexico secured its independence in the 19th century and became a key economic center and trade route between the new nation and America. Monterrey played a prominent role in the Wars of Texas Independence and afterwards when France invaded Mexico during our Civil War.

As I visited the museums of the town with its exhibits captioned in Spanish, I kept thinking of the movie *Juarez*. It depicted the French seizing the country, the establishment of Maximillian and Carlota as Emperor and Empress of Mexico, and the fight by the Mexicans to re-assert their independence.

Continuous foreign intervention, whether by America or Europe, played a key role in keeping Mexico poor and forcing its people to flee across the border to a land of hope and opportunity. After all, it was land that once belonged to them.

Toward the end of our visit I said to Colleen, "Despite the overthrow of Lili'uokalani I think we are lucky in Hawai'i that the United States became our protector. Otherwise we could have wound up just like the Mexican people constantly invaded, living in poverty, and with an unstable government."

Colleen thought for some moments then said, "Very nice people here. Many Catholic churches. Good open market place where you can buy silver ornaments, colorful blankets, clothes, belts, and many other things." Do you want to come with me? I have a guide."

"Sure," I said, following her out the door where we met a slender, light-skinned Mexican named Alonzo. He led us to a large plaza where numerous stalls were set up with tables piled high with goods and colorful blankets spread out on the ground where fat, short, dark copper-colored women sat amidst trinkets, small pillows, and silver jewelry.

"Who are these women?" I asked.

"They are Indio, natives of the Americas," Alonzo answered.

"I thought everybody in Mexico are natives."

"Not so!" Alonzo answered, anger in his voice.

"I'm sorry. I didn't realize there were differences."

"There are. You can tell by the color of the skin. The lighter the color the more pure the person is."

"Pure what?"

"Spanish of course."

"Are you Spanish?"

Alonzo sighed, "I am *mestizo*."

"What is that?"

"A Spanish and Indian mix, but I am mostly of pure blood. My father came from Spain."

"Your mother Indian?"

"No!" Alonzo spat out the word.

"Mestizo?"

"Of course, most people in Mexico are."

"Does it make a difference what color you are?"

"Yes. The dark ones live in the hills, hold no jobs, and only make money by selling in the market place like these women." Alonzo pointed to the ladies squatting on blankets.

"Those who have the money are the Spanish?"

"Yes, and mestizos like me."

Our conversation lapsed and we wandered through the market place, my sister buying goods aided by Alonzo in the bargaining. But what our guide said troubled me. The hotel was run by light-skinned men. The less white were the bell hops, room cleaners, and janitors. There were no Indios doing any of the service jobs or government work. The color of your skin made a significant difference in your social status in Mexico.

Wondering where I fit in, I asked Alonzo, "I'm half-European and half-Hawaiian, a brown person. If I lived in Mexico could I get a good job?"

Our guide shook his head, "I can't say. Maybe work in a hotel or restaurant. If you asked me about your sister, she could pass for Spanish, white skin, fine features, very high class. She would have no trouble."

I returned to the hotel realizing that discrimination existed everywhere I visited. Skin color marked you. It defined your social status, political status, and wealth. The only place where it made no difference was Kapa'a.

CHAPTER 22

Journey's End

Leaving Mexico proved difficult. We were waved through to the American side. The border guards there made it clear they did not like Mexicans. Our family name of Fernandez proved a lightning rod for inquiry as to which country we owed allegiance to. Birth certificates, identity cards, visas, insurance, auto ownership, all proved marginally acceptable. After a rigorous inspection of our vehicle, we left, thankful that we escaped jail or being sent back across the line.

As we hurried through the American southwest, I followed the news stories of the summer Olympics. A young seventeen-year-old kid was competing for America in a ten event track and field competition.

We drove to the fabled caverns of Carlsbad, New Mexico, where bats hung from the ceiling. It is an eerie experience to see thousands of brown balls sleeping above you in a cave and then waiting outside the entrance for night to come. With the dying of light, these predators arose, screeched, and flew out into the murky sky like thousands of tiny Draculas hunting for prey.

We left Carlsbad the next day. As we drove, I told my sister about the decathlon athlete at the London Olympics.

"Who is this boy?" Colleen asked.

"High school kid from Tulare, California, his name is Bob Mathias. Interesting thing about him, he recently tried all ten events in the spring of this year. Six months later he's in London, competing."

"How did he do?" Dad asked as he maneuvered our car to avoid a tumble weed rolling across the highway.

"The newspapers make it sound dramatic. It's two days of competition. On the second day heavy fog and rain made conditions miserable. At ten o'clock at night the last event occurs. Cars are driven onto the field to light the track. It's a fifteen hundred meter run. Mathias is exhausted. This is only the third time he has competed in the decathlon. He's got to win the race, but it is dark, wet, and confusing, even the officials can't see what's going on."

I paused for dramatic effect.

"What happened?" My sister said.

"Mathias won. He is the youngest person to win the decathlon."

At the time, the story of the athlete from Tulare struck a chord within me for we were about the same age. I wanted to meet him, but I thought a kid from Hawai'i would never get close to such a celebrity. I was wrong.

After Carlsbad, we stopped in Los Angeles to visit the La Brea tar pits. In pre-historic times animals sank into the methane-saturated ooze and were preserved. We didn't see any fossils of dinosaurs, but there were skeletons of mastodons, wolves, tigers, and other predators.

Exhausted from a two month trip, we pulled into the garage of our three-story Victorian. Unpacked and showered, I settled down to read the newspapers, enjoying Herb Caen who wrote with wit and sarcasm about the social happenings in San Francisco.

A story line told of a new nation, carved out of Palestine. After centuries of persecution and the asphyxiation of six million by the Nazis, the Jews found a home. A call went out for all those who believed in Jehovah to come to Israel and be safe. But the Muslims denounced the British for permitting "non-believers" to desecrate the Holy Land. They threatened their eradication.

Dad interrupted my reading saying, "My teacher wants to meet you. I'll be in school in the morning and introduce you."

"School, what are you learning?"

"Grammar, penmanship, typing, and arithmetic."

"You're retired, why not enjoy life?"

"I only got to the third grade before my father put me to work. I need to learn to be a better person."

"But you're a successful business man. You own a big movie theater."

"All my life I regretted not having a good education. I got cheated too many times because I didn't understand. That's why you should become an attorney."

From my earliest days I wanted to be a good fisherman like my Hawaiian grandfather who mom loved very much. Kamehameha Schools' focus for years had been training male students to be blue collar workers and women to be homemakers. When I entered, a college curriculum designed for a few students had begun. But I was placed in the C class for future manual laborers. Somehow I fought my way into the A class, but until my junior year my grades were not outstanding.

"I don't have the ability to be an attorney."

"You must try hard. I need you to take over the business. After dinner we will go for a walk."

Once supper ended, my dad took us to visit Golden Gate Park. He loved this stroll along Haight Street past Ashbury to the edge of the thousand acres of trees and flowers that bordered the west end of San Francisco. Within lighted stone kiosks I watched dozens of old men playing chess or checkers.

"All these folks are retired," my dad said. "Is this what you want me to do? Is this what you want to be when you are old?"

He made a challenging statement, but I felt resentful. I had been left with relatives for half of my life and fended for myself without help or guidance. Should I let myself be pushed around to do something I had no interest in?

I remained silent.

At night the park is beautiful. Wisps of fog float through the trees giving it a mysterious witching appearance. I hiked through the grass until I got a call to return home. Jogging ahead, my mind whirled over a myriad of thoughts.

On our trip I had learned a lot about America. How it had become a nation by eradicating native people. How immigrants, enticed by the claim of "All men are created equal and have the right to life, liberty, and the pursuit of happiness," found after arrival that they were discriminated against. How blacks and browns were the despicable ones to be beaten or lynched for the slightest transgressions. That religious intolerance which had driven the Pilgrims to America still existed in our country.

Maybe I should return to Kaua'i, bury my head in the sand like an ostrich, and block out all the bad things I had learned about. What should I do?

As my dad promised he took me to his school the next day. At Golden Gate College, seniors received an education they had been deprived of.

My father insisted that my mother go to school also. Her education had lasted to the third grade before her father put her to work to make money and send his adult sons to Honolulu to receive university level training.

"This is my teacher, Mr. Goldstein," Dad said, introducing a slender man whose thin white hair barely covered his scalp. His spectacles, perched on a long nose, and the pencil set on his ear made me think of Dickens's Bob Cratchit.

"This is my son, William, who I told you about."

"It is grand to meet you. I've heard all about you. President of everything there is to be president of in Honolulu."

His words embarrassed me and I said nothing.

"Your father and mother are in school here. They have learned a great deal," Goldstein continued without waiting for an answer. "Your parents told me that they wanted your sister and you to have the education they never had. When your father described your achievements I knew that there is only one university you must go to."

Goldstein's eyes peered at me over his glasses. I knew he expected me to say something so I said, "Where is that?"

"Stanford University, it's thirty miles south of here, in a town called Palo Alto. You must see it."

I felt trapped into something I didn't want to do. But what was the choice, become a somebody or remain a nobody? Still unsure, but realizing I didn't want to hurt my parents, I said, "That sounds good."

William Antonne and Agnes Scharsch Fernandez at Stanford University
Palo Alto, CA, 1948. (Family photograph)

"It's settled then. I'll give your father directions and off you go."

The next day we traveled to the university. It was awesome. Light yellow sandstone buildings everywhere. A large tower named after President Hoover, and a chapel with a beautiful fresco on the outside façade.

School was not in session so we easily toured the campus. I loved the farm-like atmosphere of the school.

"I would be so proud if you went to Stanford," my mother said.

That evening I packed to return home to Hawai'i. A fog horn blared from the radio in the kitchen. I heard the announcer say, "The Adventures of Sam Spade."

My favorite character actor, Howard Duff said, "Type a letter, Effie."

For the next half-hour I became absorbed in Dashiell Hammett's ace detective solving a murder. The series intrigued me, for, like Sherlock Holmes, Spade could gather facts, analyze them, and come up with answers. Could I do as good a job in analyzing the facts thrust upon me? What I had learned on our trip? The desire my parents had for me to be educated and Goldstein's recommendation of Stanford contrasted with an inner desire to escape achievement and live the stress free life of a fisherman.

A big ulu I speared. (Family photograph)

CHAPTER 23

Return to Hawai'i

"Get up you slobs!" J. Akuhead Pupule yelled. He gave the time of day followed by bells, buzzes, and whistles on KGMB. His real name is Hal Lewis but he changed it when an irate listener called in and said, "Hey, you *Pupule Akuhead* (crazy fishhead)! You got the time wrong." I liked the radio disc jockey because he was zany, came from San Francisco, and played great music in the morning.

As I got ready for the school day, Aku started the Hawaiian War Chant, *"Tahuwai la a tahuwai wai la…"* It is a catchy tune and I began to hum it thinking of my new-found passion, a search for the causes of war. It was kicked off when the family visited Fields Department Store in Chicago. On the third floor there was a display of Britain's toy soldiers. Ever since the movie *Gunga Din* I had been intrigued by the rise of the British Empire. Now it appeared to be falling apart with India going for independence and other former colonies seeking self-governance.

I bought a set of Bengal Lancers because of another movie. This decision started a desire to learn more about wars why they occur, how they are won, and why other wars started after a victory. More to the point, Kamehameha was an ROTC school, and if conflict came students believed we would be first to go into the military as had happened on December 7, 1941.

Marching to the assembly hall with my other classmates there was speculation as to the purpose of our gathering. "Some military officers are coming to test us," Roy said.

"About what?" Gino asked.

"Not sure, maybe about joining the army," Roy answered.

"Don't want to go. I'm going to be a Beach Boy," Gino said.

"So you can *ho'omalimali* the *wahine* tourists and get into their pants," I said.

"Who me? I wouldn't do something like that," Gino answered with a smile.

"I know you," Roy said. "You're the biggest bull-shitter in town."

We laughed and entered the assembly hall. There were three military officers on stage along with the school's PMS&T, Professor of Military Science and Tactics. A buzz developed in the room as students whispered: "They're going to tell us to join the army."

"We just ended a big war. This is peacetime. No way will I do it," Gino said.

"I think those officers on stage are going to tell us that big trouble is coming. The Communists are taking over the world," I said.

"Don't know about that," Gino answered. "But I want to have some fun in life like my uncle on the beach."

The PMS&T called the assembly to order and introduced the military on stage. A colonel stepped to the podium. He talked about World War II history and how appeasement hadn't stopped the Germans from starting a war in Europe. He spoke about the rise of the Japanese Empire, their invasion of China, and the attack on Pearl Harbor. Then he asked this question, "What is happening in Europe today?"

Silence,

I could see our PMS&T squirming in his chair. He had not taught us current events. Somewhat foolishly I raised my hand. "The Berlin Blockade by the Russians is causing our country and West Europe to fear a Communist takeover. There is talk of forming an organization for defense."

"That is correct," the colonel said.

I saw our PMS&T relaxing. He gave me a nod. The colonel spoke about the formation of a North Atlantic Treaty Alliance and explained the idea of containing Russia. But then he switched to the Far East. "Where will the United Nations face its greatest challenge in Asia?

The room remained silent.

Both the colonel and our PMS&T searched for someone to answer. I sensed gloom descending on our school's military staff. A minute passed in silence. Our commander looked around the room, settling his eyes on me. I did the un-cool thing and raised my hand.

At first I wasn't called on, but there were no other volunteers and the colonel pointed to me.

"After the war, Russia occupied North Korea, and the United States occupied South Korea. A line was drawn at the 38th parallel dividing the two countries. Both Russia and America are withdrawing. We are turning over control of South Korea to the United Nations. The new president of North Korea has vowed to invade the south and unify the country."

There were smiles from our military staff as the colonel acknowledged my answer is correct. He went on to explain the dangers of the Red menace. "All of China is falling to the Communists. Half the world is under the control or influence of the Soviet Union. You young men must be prepared to do your part in keeping the rest of what is left, free and democratic."

Then the colonel went into the hard sell, "You in the ROTC must continue your training at the university level. You must become officers in a rebuilt army and navy that will fight Communism and stop it from taking over the world."

His appeal to patriotism did not receive an enthusiastic response from my classmates. I think many of us were stunned by his proposal. One war had ended and another war appeared to be on its way.

My friends and I huddled afterward to discuss what we should do. "Once I graduate I'm heading to Alaska where no one will find me," my cousin Buddy said.

"No way to escape by going there. It's still a part of America. You have to leave all U.S. territory to avoid the draft," Roy said.

"Draft, I thought it ended after the war," Buddy said.

"Yeah, but Congress made it law again last year. Everyone 18 to 25 has to register," I said.

"How do you know about all this? How did you come up with those answers?" Gino asked.

"I read the newspapers every day. You got to know what's going on. Otherwise we could be caught again with our pants down like it happened at Pearl Harbor."

"The Beach Boy life is what I want. Not fighting somebody," Gino said.

"But if there is war, you'll get drafted. Maybe you ought to go to UH and become an officer," Roy said.

"I don't think I have the grades to make it into the University of Hawai'i."

"Yeah, most of us wouldn't get in. It's all shop, shop, shop," Roy said.

My classmate had hit the nail solidly on its head. Kamehameha was orientated to giving out high school diplomas, then casting their graduates out onto the open labor market to be day laborers.

"If you stay in Hawai'i," Buddy said, "you got no place to go except the police department or the telephone company."

"Or pumping gas," Roy interrupted. "I guess Hawaiians are lucky we got an education from the Princess. If we stayed in public schools none of us would graduate."

Roy's cynicism was right on, especially for kids from the outer islands. "Maybe the thing to do is get your diploma, join the service, and work your way up in the military," I said.

"Not smart. Officers come from West Point or college graduates, not guys like us. We are just cannon fodder to fight in the front lines," Roy said sarcasm in his voice.

"In combat, it's best not to be an officer. At Bunker Hill the orders were to pick off the British commanders first," I said.

"Break it up. Go back to class," a faculty member ordered.

Revelations from the morning were not the only jolt I received that day. In afternoon class discussion about going to college became a hot button topic. When it came my turn to speak I said, "I plan to apply to Stanford University."

"Stanford!" my teacher snorted. "You'll be lucky to get into the University of Hawai'i."

All of the educators at Kamehameha were recruited from the U.S. mainland. I felt that some held a dim view of Hawaiians. Fortunately there were others that believed in us. My family had accumulated enough money from the Roxy Theater to pay for a college education. But I was uncertain as to what I wanted to do. I decided to chat with Buddy about going to Alaska.

CHAPTER 24

A Glorious Summer

The Na Pali coastline on the north shore of Kaua'i.

A graduation from high school should be one of the great moments in life. It signals a change from childhood into adulthood. But like millions of young people everywhere, we faced an uncertain future. Adding to the dilemma was the rising power of Communism. It threatened to engulf the world in war and place young men at risk of fighting and dying on foreign soil.

On the mainland, the House Un-American Activities Committee made this question one of the most feared ever asked: "Are you now or have you ever been a member of the Communist Party?" Threatened by unionism, the Big Five used the terror of the Red menace to squash the ILWU and its leaders. They requested Congressional hearings in Hawai'i to ask that question and uncover the communist influences that they claimed caused strikes and disrupted business.

Continuing education was an option for young men. But college scholarships were not available. On graduation, fifty dollars was my gift. Many in the class received nothing. A few boys intended to go to the University of Hawai'i. The women of the Class of 1949 looked forward to marriage and homemaking. That is what they had been trained for.

I took a small coastal steamer back to Kaua'i. It's a beautiful nighttime trip. O'ahu lies mysterious in the late evening as you leave port and far to the north is the dark bulk of the Garden Island. Below deck, there is set of rooms for passengers. They are double-bunked and cramped, but large enough to hold all the goods I had accumulated over my five years at Kamehameha.

Moses, a classmate from Kaua'i, shared a room with me. We swapped stories before bedding down. "Don't know what to do," he said. "Maybe try long line-fishing with my uncle. What you going to do?"

"Not sure," I answered. "Want to fish like you, but dad wants me to be a lawyer."

"That's hard. Think you can do it?"

"Don't know. One of our teachers laughed when I told him."

"That's the trouble with some of those mainland guys, they think Hawaiians are dumb. Show him you can do it."

"I got to get into college first."

Conversation ended and we went to sleep. I woke early and headed onto the deck. The south end of my island loomed ahead. Flying fish skimmed along the water gliding like winged torpedoes over the waves. A pod of dolphins raced to us and arced in front of the ship like wheels on a child's tricycle churning through a shallow pond. Their graceful movements guided us into Port Allen.

Spinner dolphins leap among the waves.

My cousin Alice greeted me and took me to a truck which I loaded with my possessions from school. I rode in the bed of the vehicle, jostled, and bouncing with every bump in the road. Wisps of clouds hid mountain peaks. The sky slowly brightened shading into denim blue as the minutes passed and we got closer to Kapa'a. Eagerness swelled inside me as I watched the ocean rolling into shore. It was a stunning morning, a great day to go diving.

Arriving at Alice's cottage, which my dad and I had helped build, I spied her husband Jack standing by his model T-Ford preparing to go to work. "Bill," he said, "When I get back I have a surprise for you."

"Can I borrow one of your spears?" I asked.

"Don't lose it in a big fish."

"I'll whack him in the head. That is sure to make him go crazy."

We laughed.

I watched Jack drive off, unpacked my gear, found my diving bag, retrieved a spear, and headed for the sea. Illuminated in the rising light, long waves rolled into shore. They were not high enough for surfing, but ideal for spear fishing.

In front of me a cannery waste pipe held above the water by rock pilings, was not pouring garbage into the ocean. Pineapple grinding had not begun. When it occurred thousands of gallons of unwanted yellow juice, leaves, and rind would spout from its mouth, clouding the water and filling the ocean with debris. This dumping made it difficult for swimmers and fishermen, but that was okay. The cannery employed hundreds of people and gave me a summer job. Kapa'a town could not exist without it.

Some distance from shore a head bobbed in and out of the water. With a shallow dive, I skimmed through the sea, kicking up small geysers of foam. It is said that Duke Kahanamoku set his world records because of long, wide, duck like-feet. That's what I needed to push myself through the sea.

A puffer fish, its yellow and black fins fluttering, hovered in the water staring with its Little Bo Peep eyes. Trying to avoid it, I aroused its ire. Within moments it sucked in water, tripling in size. Quills thrust out like dozens of sharp nails prepared to fend off an attack. Some people say that a prick can cause death. I don't know, but it's best not to disturb the critter. I swam away.

A low shelf encrusted with coral sprouts acted as a home for dozens of small green and black-striped *manini*. They swam around it then darted inside. Within moments they floated out to see if the danger had gone away. Once the lidless eyes with the round yellow rim around the irises spotted me, they fled back into their hiding place. A pair of Moorish idols with their dorsal fins trailing like a whip from their disk-shaped bodies nibbled at seaweed growing on the rocks.

What a wonderful place to be in. An endless pond filled with a multitude of wonders. I felt like Aladdin when he entered the cave of the thieves. This is home. The warm water is comforting, caressing, and wipes troubles away. For hours I swam, fishing a little, but mostly enjoying the relief from stress.

When I returned to the house, Jack was there. "I have a surprise," he said.

From a shed he drew out a long black net.

"Good looking throw net," I said.

"It's yours."

"I don't know how to use it."

"I'll show you."

Jack proceeded to fold the seven foot tall mesh into threes, draped one portion over his left shoulder, and with his right hand holding the lead line, twisted, and hurled the net onto the grass in a perfect circle. "You try," he said.

For an hour I did, flubbing at first, then eventually understanding the turning of the hips, shoulders, and casting out the net. By supper time I was tolerable. "In the early morning we go to the ocean," Jack said.

At first light, we headed for the sea. Poised on the rocks overlooking the ocean, Jack said, "You must look through the water to see the fish. Be patient. Wait until they group together. Then it is all timing as you twist back, and go forward heaving the net."

We marched along the shore until Jack made a cautionary sign. He folded the net along his shoulders, bent low, moved forward and threw. Not a bad haul, five fish.

I tried, but messed the net up in my eagerness. After a couple of misses, Jack said, "I need to go to work. You must practice."

A throw net fisherman casts his net at a group of fish.

We went home and for the rest of the day I tried to master the art. While I worked at it, my cousin Alice took a call, then said, "You want to see Ni'ihau?"

This is the Forbidden Island seventeen miles west of Kaua'i. It has been owned by the Robinson family since the 19th century when Elizabeth Sinclair purchased it from the Kingdom of Hawai'i. It is called forbidden since no one is allowed on it. In its seventy square miles, several hundred Hawaiians live in the old way, speaking the ancient language used by the people before the missionaries came.

"Oh, yes," I answered.

"Jack arranged with a fish spotter to take you on his airplane around the island and then fly to Ni'ihau."

I forgot about net fishing and found a map of the island and some of its history. A single volcano built it five million years ago. Because it lies in Kaua'i's rain shadow the island has been plagued by droughts. There are no running streams. Rain water when it comes is caught in shallow lakes. When Captain James Cook stumbled on Ni'ihau in 1778 he noted that it was treeless. Over their years of ownership, the Robinsons planted thousands of trees helping to increase rainfall.

Ni'ihau Island just off the western coast of Kaua'i. It is called "The Forbidden Island" because it is privately owned. (Courtesy of Kaua'i Historical Society)

It has a fragile economy. The owners grow and sell sheep, cattle, honey, and kiawe charcoal. Its beaches produce wondrous shells. The shell leis of Ni'ihau are world famous.

After the attack on Pearl Harbor, a Japanese pilot crash-landed on the island. For three days he terrorized it before he was killed along with a Japanese-American citizen who aided him. An interesting, little-known fact is President Roosevelt considered it as a location for the United Nations.

Excitement kept me awake for hours. I had only seen Ni'ihau's profile from the top of the western mountains of Waimea. This would be my chance to visit an island few had ever been to. Kaua'i was in shadow when Jack rocked me awake. We drove to the air field, met the pilot, strapped in, and flew into the sky.

The airplane was a vintage Piper Cub with its trademark yellow hue painted from end to end and wing tip to wing tip. During World War II it was the primary training aircraft for future pilots. Light and maneuverable it could land and take off from any terrain that is flat, treeless, and without boulders.

Tex, the pilot, said, "We got to find fish. We fly around Kaua'i looking for *akule*. Then we go Ni'ihau."

"You can have a *hukilau* (pull net fishing) on Ni'ihau? I thought you can't go on the island? How do you pull in the net?"

"I know Robinson's claim they own all the land, shoreline, all the way into the sea. I think they are wrong, but we don't challenge them. We do seine net fishing with a purse to haul them in."

"What?"

"When you see a big school of fish out in the deep, you surround them hukilau style. But instead of hauling the fish to shore you draw up the lead line until all the fish are held in a purse. Our boat comes and with small nets we scoop the fish in."

"Wow, that is great. You can do it anywhere. What's going to happen to guys like Uncle John who pull net from the shore?"

"Right now plenty akule to catch. But someday all gone. We are starting to take our boats out to French Frigate Shoals. Good fishing there."

These low-lying reefs and sand bars are five hundred miles from Hawai'i. They got their name from a French explorer who almost smashed his two frigates into the submerged rocks of the atoll. The shoals are a crescent-shaped reef sitting on an eroded volcano. Within its circle are small sand islets. They are a navigation hazard since much of the atoll is submerged. Along its fringes, fishing is awesome. During the war the Japanese used it as a refueling harbor and anchorage for their long-range flying boats. Scientists claim that someday all of Hawai'i will be atolls.

"I hear the long line fishing is great at the shoals," I said.

"Best place if you want big tuna," Tex answered.

"You think I can go there?"

"I don't know. Ask your uncle."

Our left wingtip dipped and the Piper Cub descended toward the sea. Tex dove so fast, my stomach felt like it leaped into my chest. "That is scary," I said.

"I thought I saw fish," Tex answered. "Look over there, the dark spot in the sea."

"Don't see a thing."

"We're flying right over it."

"Yeah, I see it. Maroon and very wide. It's a big school. Shall we tell Uncle John? They're coming into his bay."

"You can do it when you get back."

Our airplane swooped up and over the Princeville hills. Beyond our windshield unfolded magnificent Hanalei. At the far end of the valley a half-dozen waterfalls cascaded down the mountain side feeding a lazy river flowing aimlessly past the Princeville heights and into the sea. In the far distance the peak of Makena marked the end of the government road and the beginning of the winding trail around the Na Pali Coast.

Hanalei Bay, Mt. Makena. The Na Pali Coast State Park trail begins there.

"Hawaiians sacrificed virgins to the shark god by throwing them off that mountain," Tex said, a smile lighting his face.

"I never heard that story. Only know about the Hula School below Makena dedicated to goddess Laka."

"Maybe you're right. Hawaiians did throw fire sticks from it at night."

"My aunt told me about how beautiful the fire fall was."

We sped past the bay and headed into Ha'ena. Below the airplane lay the gorgeous sand beach of Lumahai. It is treacherous. Currents will sweep a swimmer out to sea and the waves create an undertow that sucks you to the bottom and holds you there.

We flew by the caves, lava tubes that no longer spewed forth magma. Inside its caverns are ancient burial sites. Beware if you take anything from them. A ghost may come in the night to haunt you.

Our Piper Cub soared by the towering cliffs of the Na Pali coast. Somewhere in its many valleys it is claimed there exists a lost tribe. Legend has it that if you fall into their hands you will be sacrificed to the god Ku.

Kalalau Valley, Na Pali Coast

As we sped by Kalalau Valley Tex said, "See all those white spots along the rocks? Wild goats. They are a big nuisance."

"Any good to eat?"

"Real smelly. You got to soak the meat in soy sauce and ginger to take the game taste away."

"Anybody hunt them?"

"Yes. With no natural enemies, they multiply real fast. So you got to shoot 'em to keep the animals from destroying the scenery."

We flew by a valley with a long white sand beach and a reef surrounding it. "Beautiful place," I said.

"Miloli'i, great hunting and fishing. Try it sometime."

It looked like a perfect spot to hide from the world. "How can you get into it? Is there a trail over the mountains?"

"You take a boat. At the edge of the reef you jump in and swim to shore. Or you can fly in."

Ni'ihau Island became visible. From afar, it looked like the iron ship Monitor sitting motionless on the sea. Strange I thought that, maybe it's because I knew that the island had been purchased at the time of the American Civil War.

Tex's Piper Cub drew closer to the Forbidden Island. It began to take shape. I saw a central mountain mass splaying out north and south into lower ground. Everything about the island appeared primeval. There was not a building or human anywhere. On the flat ground to the north of the mountain were shallow lakes.

"That's where the animals come to drink," Tex said. "On the other side the Hawaiians have big tanks where they catch rain water. When it is drought time they have to come to Kaua'i."

Our airplane lost altitude. "Are we out of gas?"

"No, just going to land and stretch out."

This was exciting, trespassing on Robinson property. The Piper glided smoothly to a stop on the sparsely grassed surface of Ni'ihau. Hopping out of the airplane, I looked for a posse of angry Hawaiians to come charging out of the unseen folds in the land to nab us.

"Don't worry," Tex said. "The village is miles away. There are no telephones, power lines, or automobiles. There are horses, but you can see their dust from a long way off."

I walked around the airplane studying everything. What was it like to own an island and be in control of hundreds of people? You could act like a feudal lord and have your minions scare up game to hunt. Make all the rules that everyone must obey. Have wild parties where no one could complain. Wow, what a life. No worries about school and getting a job.

We got back in the aircraft, bumped along the level ground, and soared into the air. Tex headed toward the village, a series of wooden houses and shacks set within a walled enclosure. Near it was a tree-lined roadway leading to a large mansion. "The Robinsons have it rich," I said. "Nice house and servants."

"It's not like that," Tex answered. "They sell animals and honey but don't make enough money to pay expenses. Hawaiians live on the island for free. The family provides them with food and transport to Kaua'i. No servants. Robinsons take care of themselves. They are good to the people and want to preserve their old way of life."

I remained silent thinking of what I saw. Far to the northwest lay Japan. The Empire had sent a fleet seven-and-a-half years ago to attack Hawai'i. One of the enemy pilots crashed on Ni'ihau, and terrorized the island for three days before he was killed. I wondered where below me all this had taken place. What this event proved is that nowhere can you escape from war.

Our airplane banked for home. It had been a smooth flight. I had seen fish and would tell Uncle John about it. Tex would report to his boss the large school of *akule* he spotted off of Ni'ihau.

The next morning Cousin Alice said, "Your father wants you to earn money for college by working at the theater,"

I remained silent, tired of being told what to do by grown-ups. Maybe it was time to contact Cousin Buddy and see if he still wanted to go to Alaska. He had said, "That's the coming territory where a young guy can make his fortune."

"You can work to mid-afternoon and then go fishing and we have some nice surprises for you," Alice interrupted my day dreaming.

Her statements changed my mood considerably. I wanted to practice with the throw-net and spearfish with my friends. Plus, I wondered what the surprises were. "What are you thinking of?"

"Ask Jack tonight."

I worked on theater seats all day, went swimming after, and hurried home for supper eager to find Alice's husband. He had returned from work and was in the kitchen frying steaks.

"Howzit?" I said trying to appear nonchalant, but dying to find out the surprises.

"What are you doing?"

"Painting," I didn't say more for it was not the style to make demands. Let the elders do the talking.

"Hear from any colleges?"

Questions, questions, I thought. Let's get to the important stuff. But I restrained myself saying, "I got accepted to Rutgers and University of Redlands. California turned me down, said I was from out of state. No word from Stanford."

"Do you remember Bobby at the repair shop in town?"

"Yeah. He's a great guy. I go over there to make my spears and talk story."

"He asked if you wanted to go to Miloli'i."

"Yes. When?"

"This Friday and Saturday."

My wish had come true. From the air the isolated valley along the Na Pali coast intrigued me. Could someone escape from the world, live in the valley and survive? This was my chance to find out. But more important, it promised adventure.

Friday morning we loaded Tex's Piper Cub with a Springfield 1906 rifle, my spear fishing equipment, and a twenty pound throw net. "What's this for?" I asked Bobby.

My friend is a short, thin, Japanese guy without muscles. His hair was sparse and cut short. His thin lips curved up into a wry smile as he said, "To catch *moi*."

"You're too small to throw this thing."

"But you are six feet. You can catch them."

"No way. I'm just learning and this is twice as heavy as my black net."

"You can do it," Bobby said his lips breaking into a wide grin.

"I'll try," I answered as Tex took off.

Once in the air, I wondered where we could land. Miloli'i sits in a half circle of mountain. Its edges that meet the sea are high stone walls. Its earth floor is rock strewn and uneven.

Na Pali Coast scene

"There is no airfield. How are we going to get off this airplane?" I asked.

"Not to worry," Bobby said.

"Maybe we should have taken a boat?"

"We would have gotten to the valley at night and had to swim in. This is the best deal."

I became silent, unwilling to express my fear. This is a new adventure. I prayed it didn't end badly.

We flew past Kalalau Valley and another next to it and approached the northerly face of Miloli'i. "Where are we going to put down?" I said, looking at an irregular rock- strewn landscape.

"That beach," Tex said nodding his head toward the shore.

Below our aircraft lay a narrow ribbon of sand the length of a football field. The slender light yellow strip of dead coral ended in a rock wall several hundred feet high. Tex flew past the landing area, banked the Piper Cub around and descended.

Miloli'i Beach

To my right the wing of our aircraft barely skimmed past a steep cliff strewn with a talus field of round rocks. I could see at its topmost edge scores of mountain goats chewing on the grass struggling through the stone. They paid scant attention to the rumble of our engine as its noise echoed from the rock walls.

As we began our approach, through the airplane's windshield I saw a wall of stone growing bigger as the wheels of the Piper sought hard packed sand. Our airplane's tires bumped the ground, bounced up, and then down. I saw the mountain grow huge through the glass in front of me. The engine died and only the braking action of the sand slowed our momentum. It seemed inevitable that we would crash. I crouched low. I thought I heard the smashing of metal and wood over the sound of waves rolling up the shore.

Our airplane stopped. "You can come up for air," Bobby said.

I opened my eyes, realizing I was not hurt. In front of me stood a tower of rock with tufts of grass sprouting from crevices in the stone. Our airplane was still, the propeller feathered, and within a few feet of the high cliff that anchored into the sea.

"Get your gear out," Tex said. "Got to get back to work."

Bobby and I unloaded, watched our pilot turn the Piper around, and fly into the sky.

"What do we do now?" I said.

"Put our stuff in the cottage and catch *moi*."

"With what?"

"The throw net."

"Are you going to hurl it?"

"No, you are."

"It's too heavy."

"You can do it."

After storing our gear, Bobby headed for the beach. From its edge, he studied the submerged reef looking for what Hawaiians call the king of fish. We strode together searching through the waves. Bobby stopped, pointing, "You see that hole in the green maybe five *moi* swimming around."

"I don't see anything."

"They are there. Get ready."

I folded the net in three parts and said, "This is heavy. I don't think I can do it."

"You can. I can taste the fish now."

"Where do I throw it?"

"Cover the hole. That's enough."

I made a stealthy approach watching the green reef and its irregular opening. It looked like an old lava tube. I wondered how deep it went, maybe into the island itself. I kept low, with the sun at my back. I did not want my shadow to spook the fish I couldn't see. I trusted Bobby's judgment for he kept pointing the direction I should take.

He motioned me to stop. I rose up, and started my throw.

I twisted, turned, and hurled with all the power I could muster. Unfortunately the heaviness of the net made my movements clumsy so the net failed to open in a perfect circle. Instead, a portion of the lead weights clung together pulling mesh out in a long string that chunked into the water with a loud splash scaring the fish into the hole in the reef.

"You lost our supper," Bobby said.

As I gathered up the tangled strings and lead, my friend goaded me again for my failure, "Too bad. We have nothing to eat."

Bobby's whining stung me. Why had he brought such a heavy net that even he couldn't throw? We knew at the start of our trip that we must live off the land like the ancient people. Tex's Piper Cub could only carry three and some hunting equipment. Miloli'i did not have growing crops or a grocery store.

I smothered my irritation and said, "Not to worry, I have my spear."

I gave my friend the net, retrieved my fishing equipment, and dove into the water. It was clear, translucent, and cool. Absent was cannery waste or junk that the plantations dumped into the sea. I could see a long way underwater until my vision ended in a distant wall of blue. Fish swam around me, munching on coral rocks or just floating with the waves. Oddly shaped stones rose from the ocean floor. They were jagged and twisted as if the hot lava when it plunged into the salt water leaped up and froze in place.

I watched for *mano*. Fishermen said that the southwest edge of the Na Pali coast is the spawning and birthing place of sharks. My only defense against the predator was a slender six foot spear.

I saw *uhu* (parrot fish) flitting along the reef. Their beak is similar to that of the jungle bird and their faces are blunt.

I dove a distance away and began to stalk using the cover of rocks to keep my body hidden. Calculating that I had swum far enough, I floated above the sheltering reef, my spear poised. A school of blue and red parrot fish crunched coral in front of me. I pulled back my Hawaiian sling and let loose, striking a blue uhu in the center of its body.

Twisting, turning, smashing into stones, the fish fought to free itself of the tormenting shaft that pierced its side. Before it could find a hole to slide into, I grasped the haft of my spring steel rod and hauled the animal in.

Threading it onto my stringer I surfaced and watched below. The school returned to the spot it had vacated. I breathed, dove, cocked my spear, and kicked hard. A red fish startled by my plunge tried to escape. I skewered it from the top through to the bottom of his body. It wobbled and dropped to the reef.

It wasn't long before I had enough uhu and swam to shore. Seeing my prizes, Bobby said, "Okay, we eat tonight."

We headed for the caretaker's cottage and met Dickey. He was older than me by a few years, white, blond, and athletic. He had been living in the valley for a week and was due to leave by boat the next day.

"I love it here," Dickey said. "No cars or people, quiet nights. It is heaven on earth."

I bathed in a stream, exhilarated by the cold water and what my new friend had said. Turning to the horizon I watched the colors change from gold to crimson red and finally shades of bluish-grey as night mantled the sky. A cool breeze played over my skin making me shiver. In the fading light, a campfire sprung up. Soon fish sizzled in a pan.

In this primitive valley, a feeling of peace came over me. This is the good life. Living in my birthday suit, fishing for what I needed, and avoiding the stresses of an uncivilized world.

After supper, Dickey made the day even more enjoyable when he said, "Going torch fishing, want to come?"

With two gas lanterns and each of us armed with a trident we hiked for the rocks at the south end of the valley. In the inlets and crevices of the shallow sea, our torches revealed swarms of fish floating in the water.

Dickey pulled back his spear. He paused for a moment. Sputtering light silhouetted his body. In the darkness, he looked like a Roman *Retiarius*, a spearman, poised to strike a reclining foe. The trident flew, piercing a large red fish.

"Don't stand there," Dickey shouted. "Get them."

I flung my spear, but only hit rock. I had not accounted for the bending light effect of the water.

Bobby skewered another big red one, tossing it on the shore to flop in the *naupaka* (beach plant) that edged the sand. Dickey scrambled over stones, the torch harnessed to his body casting yellow light on the water. "Wait up," I called. But my new friend didn't pause in his work, striking fish and tossing each one into the shrubbery.

"Don't try to keep up with him," Bobby said. "I'm already bushed by this jumping from stone to stone."

I slowed and spotted a fish in the water, its disc-shaped silvery body glinting in the artificial light of the lantern flame above my head. I aimed high, taking refraction into account, flung my trident, and succeeded. Like a reaper in a hay field, I flung the spear handle up and over onto the shrubs.

Ahead, I saw Dickey fighting with a large octopus, its tentacles writhing in the dim light like snakes wiggling over his body.

"Bite the eyes," I yelled.

"He knows," Bobby said, "but he can't get to the head, we better help him."

I scrambled to Dickey. The body of the creature wrapped around his arm. Tentacles probed his face, one sucking around his mouth and another reaching into his nose like a worm exploring a hole.

Dickey fought with his hands to keep the creature from suffocating him. But the slimy arms of the beast proved difficult to grasp.

I seized a bunch of oozing flesh, slid my fingers between my friend's arm and the body of the creature, and bit. Salty excretions filled my mouth. Chewing the rubbery meat, I searched for the nerve center between the octopus's eyes. My teeth found something hard. Like a crazed dog, I clamped my jaws and pulled.

I felt something break. Tentacles stopped sucking on Dickey. They drew back from his face curling into a ball around its beak. Paralyzed, the large creature slid onto the dark boulders at my feet.

"How come you didn't spear that big thing?" I said.

Dickey gave me a weak smile and said, "I thought I could tickle it and catch it with my hands."

"That's how Hawaiians do it, but I guess you don't know the trick."

"Do you?"

"I don't want to try it, seeing what happened to you."

We laughed at the adventure that could have ended in a disaster.

Bobby interrupted saying, "I think I see turtles in the next pond."

We hiked over the rocks to where he pointed. Two big dark brown shells were wedged into a shelf in the reef.

"No way to catch them," I said.

"Take my torch," Dickey answered.

He hopped over rocks and into the water. I thought he had gone crazy. "Leave them," I said.

"Come over here and shine the torch on this one," Dickey answered.

With its head and half its body shoved into a shallow cavern in the reef, it appeared that the turtle did not sense my friend's approach. But what is his plan? The creature is big, maybe two hundred pounds. With surprising quickness, Dickey dove, reached the animal, seized it on its sides protruding from the shelf, and pulled.

Out from its hiding place scrambled the creature its four wings flapping. Avoiding its powerful beak that could bite off an arm, Dickey aimed the animal's head up. Man and beast broke the surface, the turtle's front flippers beating air. The two at the tail end churned the sea, but only succeeded in keeping half of the animal's body above the water and helping Dickey push it to the rocks where I stood.

"Grab him," Dickey yelled.

That is easy to say, but hard to do. Flippers beat like the wings of a trapped bird. The animal's beak snapped. It brought fear to my mind. I had watched a land turtle bite a leafy branch and never let go until he devoured it.

"Watch your fingers," Bobby said a grin widening his lips, revealing his teeth yellowed by smoking.

"You grab it."

"Not me, I don't like turtle meat."

"Do something," Dickey yelled, struggling to keep the head of the animal in the air. He managed to shove its rear onto stones at the water line. Fortunately the sea was calm, no waves to make our venture more difficult.

I seized a front flipper, pulled and pulled again. The turtle came out of the pond. It flapped on the rocks trying to work back into the sea. Dickey flipped it over onto its back, ending the battle.

"Enough for one night," Bobby said.

Dickey shoved the turtle further up the shore and tethered it. We gathered our fish and octopus and headed for the caretaker's cottage.

Lying on a blanket spread over the wooden floor of the building, I gazed at the stars through an open window. I felt exhausted by the efforts of the day. But the blueness of the heavens with its distant twinkling lights drew my mind back in time to those early voyagers who used the stars to guide them as they challenged the sea in search of adventure and a new land. I thought, "This is what I want, to live like my ancestors and pioneer in the wilderness." I went to sleep.

Cave with waterfall.

Bobby roused me. It was dark.

"What's up?"

"It's time to hunt. Tex will come in the early afternoon."

Grumbling about his prodding that had ended a beautiful dream, I dressed and followed him out the door. "Where are we going?"

"Over to the landing field."

We hiked toward the north end of the valley. When we reached the wide-spread talus pile that I had seen the previous day, dawn's light streamed over the mountains.

"We are going to climb those round rocks up to the goats. You take the rifle," Bobby said handing me the gun.

I looked at the pile of stones that spread like a giant black fan down the mountain side. Some of the stones were small and round like golf balls, others as big as footballs. The angle of our climb was at least forty degrees, getting steeper as you reached the top most rocks.

"Won't we slip and slide?"

"Better to climb up the pile then try to hike up the steeper sides."

Unsure of his wisdom I struggled upward, my feet searching for anchored rocks. Any stumble could start an avalanche of stone and propel me downhill like a bowling ball rolling over agates. It became more dangerous the higher we climbed for the incline of the mountain increased as the jumble of round stones decreased.

"Don't look down," Bobby said as he caught me glancing below. "Face up. Look for the goats."

The small animals I had seen on the cliff the day before took shape into large creatures with wicked-looking horns sprouting from their heads. They ignored our presence, grazing on weeds and shrubs, unafraid of our coming.

My boot slipped on loose rocks. Falling onto my chest, stones ripped into my shirt. My body slid sideways. Below, the blue sea sparkled with light from a mid-morning sun. Our landing field, which had been a thin ribbon of sand a moment ago, grew larger in my eyes. Would this plunge down a talus pile end my life without having accomplished anything?

My fall jerked to a stop as the rifle strap dug into my arm pit. Stones continued to cascade downhill some bouncing outward and free falling toward the beach. Bobby held the gun barrel, saving me from joining an avalanche rolling down the hillside.

"Maybe we should stop and shoot," I said, my breath coming in quick gasps.

"No. We go higher."

I didn't argue. It's his rifle, he held the ammunition, and I knew he had arranged this trip to get goat meat. But more to the point, I enjoyed the danger, the thrill of climbing, and the beauty of what I saw.

We came within a football field of the goats.

"Now can we stop?"

"Higher."

Up we went to the point where the flock was huge in my eyes, each goat maybe sixty or eighty pounds. Within seventy feet of the herd, Bobby said, "Halt."

"Here's the rifle," I said taking it from my shoulder.

"No, you're going to shoot," Bobby answered handing me a clip with five rounds of .30 caliber bullets.

"I've never fired this gun before."

"Don't worry, I calibrated it myself. It's accurate. Just use the sight, line up your target, and fire. Remember: it's a bolt action."

At Kamehameha we had drilled with rifles like this. I was familiar with its weight, mechanism, and sighting bar.

I slipped the clip into its slot and chambered a round. I went prone onto the stone pile, spread my legs, and found a firm resting place for my elbows. I worked my chest and stomach into a comfortable and stable position. Lining the sight on a four-legged animal above me I breathed in, steadied myself, and slowly squeezed the trigger to avoid jerking the rifle off its target.

Nothing happened.

"Release the safety," Bobby whispered.

By now, the animals were staring at us and moving their feet getting ready to run.

Once more I aimed and squeezed the trigger. An explosion occurred, gas floated from the gun barrel. Nothing happened. I levered another round into the chamber and fired. Nothing happened. A third round, a fourth round, and a fifth, nothing happened. I couldn't believe that I missed five times.

"More ammo."

"Watch out, they're coming."

A large white ball rolled down the hill, then another, and another. I had to slide sideways to avoid being hit. There was a scramble of animals heading for higher ground. One of the goats appeared to limp as it attempted to climb. Behind it followed a young kid.

The struggling creature got to a point at the edge of a cliff where it appeared to be stymied, unable to climb or descend. Behind it huddled its small child.

"Do you have any more ammunition?" I said, thinking to end the parent's misery.

"Five rounds that is all."

But the creature took its fate into its own hands. It stared at the blue sea rolling to shore. It turned its head upward. Whether by intention or accident the animal gathered its rear legs and leaped. Out into the air it flew turning over and over as it plunged thousands of feet into the ocean an eerie cry piercing the stillness of the hills as it fell.

The goat disappeared leaving only the bleating of its child echoing through the mountains in constant repetition, "Maah, maah."

Shaken by this cry, Bobby and I gathered our prizes and slid down the talus pile. We took them to the caretaker's house where Dickey said he would float them to the boat that would take him away. As we gathered our gear, we heard the Piper Cub approaching the valley.

At the landing beach we loaded onto the airplane and Tex took off into the wind heading south. I couldn't speak and had been silent since the animal's death. As we rose above the round stones the engine noise echoed through the valley. I saw again the goat's leap and heard the scream of its child. I wondered if I could ever hunt again.

Kalalau Valley Lookout from Waimea Canyon

CHAPTER 25

Summer's End

Fishing consumed me during the hot middle months of the year. I could manipulate my work schedule to further my desire to be in the sea. Notifying Uncle John of the great school of fish I spotted from the air earned "'good boy" points with him. He promoted me to diver at the Kalihiwai hukilau. My job would be to free the surround net from coral snags or the two automobiles that the military had sunk in the bay.

This act made no sense, since these metal obstacles could not halt enemy landing boats. Maybe the navy thought that transport ships would sail into Kalihiwai Bay and transfer troops directly to shore. It was not possible.

At one time there existed a robust fishing village that spread along the beach. The tidal wave of April Fool's Day, 1946, smashed everything and swept many people out to sea.

After the disaster, Uncle John continued to keep watch on the orange hill overlooking the bay. Before the tidal wave struck, the ridge he sat on was empty of buildings. Today the hill was crowded. Survivors of the wave constructed homes on the high ground. Only boats and nets were parked at the shore line.

Amazing is the resilience of the north shore people of Kaua'i. Those still living had suffered huge losses from the tsunami. None of them fled the island. Instead, they re-built, either on higher ground or constructed elevated homes on the beach. These were not defiant acts, but rather an acceptance of the price you must pay for living off the bounty of the ocean and coping with its moments of destructive power. This love-hate relationship is why I am enamored with the sea.

John believed that 1949 would be a great year for fishing. In mid-July he called for divers.

From the orange hill I watched a maroon spot in the blotter-blue ocean scattering and clumping together. The mass of akule were doing what they usually do when predators strike, fleeing, then drawing back into a compact mass. It is the age-old notion that there is safety in numbers. What is important to fishermen is the movement of the animals into the shallower water of the bay.

For many moments John studied the approach of the akule. When satisfied they were in the capture zone he waved *ti* leaves, urging his minions with net-filled boats to head into the sea. "Go down," he said to Jack and me. "Help with the net."

We ran down the hill, donned our gear, and dove into the ocean. "You check the shallow part of the net," Jack said. "I'll go deeper."

After the surround had been completed I surveyed the net, clearing snags that impeded the pulling in of the mesh. The trapped school of fish was immense. It was so large that John ordered a second surround and then a third. He planned to keep the fish trapped for several days to avoid flooding the local markets and also give him time to arrange shipments to Honolulu.

On the second day my work continued. As I tended the nets underwater, I was startled by an immense grey body with a white underbelly bumping into the mesh where I worked. I surfaced and called to Jack, "Big shark. What do I do?"

"Push him away."

I had never been this close to mano before. All the horrors of shark attacks conjured in my thoughts. Maybe it is best to let sleeping dogs lie.

In the past I had seen sharks gliding along the bottom. You could tell they were hungry for their white underside swung back and forth like half-empty balloons. This killer's belly did not swing. It remained rigid.

It bumped into the net like a friendly dog trying to lick my hand. With bile building in my stomach and my insides wanting to evacuate, I pushed its head away.

Showing a grinning mouth filled with teeth filed to dagger points, it floated from me. I used the net like a movable battering ram, and shoved my hand against the sandpaper sharp grey side of the beast. It lazily moved into the interior of the crescent of net.

Surfacing I told Jack of my adventure.

"You lucky he was full up. When hungry that guy could eat you."

"If you wanted to fight him, where would you strike?"

"Put a spear in the gills. That's how it breathes. Shut off the oxygen, he dies. Better not to try it. Just rap him on the nose, sharks most sensitive part. Hit him hard, he runs away."

"What if he doesn't?"

"Say your prayers."

I thought I would experiment with the over-stuffed shark, but he didn't come back to the net. A call came to end work and I left the water without resolving my fear of mano.

Our catch was big. John gave us loads of fish, and paid each worker. My share equaled a week's pay at the cannery. I could live on that.

Our next call came two weeks later, but this time it was different. "We will bang-bang," Jack said as our net-laden motor boat headed for Secret Beach near the lighthouse.

Although clouds canopied the sky steel grey, it was not raining. Kilauea plantation flumed colored waste into the seas. From the shore to several hundred yards out, the ocean had turned milk-white with the discarded junk from the mill. On the beach fishermen were casting baited lines into the water and hauling in fish.

In a second boat, John waved his arms, "Head to the beach."

Once ashore he directed the unloading of net and ordered, "You four, pull it out to sea." He pointed to Jack and me and three others and said, "You guys run maybe a hundred-fifty yards. Go in the water and spread out. When I yell, hit the sea with your hands, feet make noise."

We ran then spread out in the water and waited for the signal. There was so much cane rubbish in the water I couldn't see beneath the surface. Nearby, Jack said, "Sharks like this, lots of food. They can't see what they bite. Watch out."

His broad smile made me answer back, "You're full of ho'omalimali."

But his statement whether true or a joke still worried me. If I saw a fin would I have time to see the shark's snout and strike it with my fist or flee before it bit? I waited for uncle's signal, searching the white water around me for the black sail knifing through it.

"Bang, bang," John yelled.

I hit the water with my arms. I swung my legs up and down like a drum major leading the school band or a Nazi storm trooper goose stepping. Five of us beating the water moved toward the net holders who were spread in a crescent in front of us.

It was impossible to see where I walked. More than once I stumbled over a rock into deep water and had to swim to find firm footing. Underwater bodies brushed by my legs. "Are there eels or barracuda in this slop?" I yelled.

"No worry," Jack called back. "Just hit the water. Scare them away."

As we approached the net, the fish trying to escape formed a dense pack in front of us, but there was no escape. I felt a crush of fins. Sharp spines pierced my legs. I saw moi thrashing in the water as they were squeezed into the funnel-shaped pocket in the middle of the mesh.

The net closed, and John ordered us to haul it to shore. Thousands of big fish squirmed inside the trap. Baskets were unloaded from boats, and flapping fish dumped into them. Once the net was emptied, John ordered another bang, bang further down the beach.

This time it proved to be colossal fun. Sharks seemed disinterested in the plantation sludge. There were no eels or barracuda in the first catch, nothing but beautiful silvery and grey-striped king fish.

Our next haul was huge. The newspapers reported our record catch of moi, eighteen thousand pounds. I received enough fish to pay Bobby back for my messing up at Miloli'i. Best of all, I got paid for my day's work. I loved fishing especially when it meant earning money.

Then Stanford University notified me that I was accepted. I relayed the news to my parents in San Francisco. My mother was overjoyed. But I was not. Living outdoors for the summer had proved exhilarating. Almost as good were the evenings when families got together, played music, sang, and danced.

The most stunning news of all occurred when Jack announced at dinner in late August, "This weekend a group of us are heading to Ni'ihau to spear-fish for *nenue*. Want to come?"

I choked on my food, finally managing a weak, "Yes."

Why was this offer exciting? It would be a chance to spearfish in waters that were virgin, where none had explored before. Jack and his brother Ben had lived on the island after the Ni'ihau Incident. They knew the people. I might meet pre-contact Hawaiians who lived in the ancient way. It was said that they spoke in the original tongue with t and r and not k and l that the Christian missionaries used in their recording of the Hawaiian alphabet. Their isolation meant that I might learn the culture of the first people to inhabit what Mark Twain called "The loveliest fleet of islands that lies anchored in any ocean."

In darkness on Saturday morning, we headed for Port Allen on the southern tip of Kaua'i. There I met two men, Ben, a wiry, round-faced, short haired, confirmed bachelor, Jack's brother, and Cowboy, a squat Japanese man with a thin moustache, a half-smile on his face, and mischievous eyes that twinkled when he spoke. He usually said one syllable words like "Hi, good, eat." He got his name because of his bowed legs, but my new friend had never ridden a horse. The captain of the sampan and the sheriff completed our crew.

Another view of Ni'ihau Island. (website photo)

It took a long time to cross seventeen miles of water. When we anchored a half-mile from shore the sunlight reached across the higher mountains of Kaua'i and lit the cliffs of northeastern Ni'ihau. "Go, swim in," Jack said. "The boat cannot go closer, too shallow."

Into the water I slid, my spear threaded through the tube of my Hawaiian sling in my left hand, my right stroking the sea, and my new fins kicking me through a still and translucent sea. As I swam, I thanked Jacques Cousteau for his invention of the rubber webbing that gave a diver the chance to go deep and catch elusive fish.

What I saw was not promising. The floor of the sea was pancake flat, without sand and only a minimal amount of corral sprouting from the frozen lava. I poked my head into one of the few crevices that I saw, spotted two five pound kumu and caught them. Nearby, Benny said, "No fish here. We go other side."

We rounded the north end stopping for a brief moment at Lehua Island, a rock thrusting hundreds of feet into the sky. It was streaked with dirty white drips and only usable as a home by seabirds. Fishing off of it proved dismal. I plunged fifty feet to find game in the cracks of the rock. My ears popped with an unbearable ache. My nasal passages ruptured with an audible sound.

I hit the surface next to Cowboy. "Huge pressure down there," I said.

"Yes," he answered in his usual single syllable monotone.

"Not worth it to fish by this rock."

"Plenty red fish."

"Maybe, but I'm going to Ni'ihau."

Blowing blood from my nose I swam several hundred yards to the bigger island. I was surprised to see a sudden rise from the deep blue of the channel separating Ni'ihau and Lehua onto a sand covered shelf three or four feet deep. It was perfect. My aching ears could not take any depth.

The crystal-clear, shallow water sparkled in the morning light. Shafts of silver and gold plunged like stalactites into the channel to my right. Swimming beyond the drop off, I saw nenue, alone or in pairs, wiggling through the calm water. With my ears hurting and nose bleeding from a ruptured capillary in my sinuses, I developed a method of capture that worked. I went still, bobbed like a cork, and waited while curious fish came to visit, then drew back my spear and fired.

My companions had also given up on fishing at Lehua and were spread out some distance ahead of me in deeper water. Enjoying myself, I stayed in the shallows. Stroking easily, I watched for fish. When I saw one, I stopped and went into my "bobbing like a cork'" routine. The hours flew and I caught a passel of nenue. Toward mid-afternoon I reached a shallow shelf split into a big V as if a giant axe had driven into the reef and divided it, creating a long narrow channel nearly thirty feet deep and six feet wide. I decided to follow it into more open water. Ahead, I could see a large underwater amphitheater.

To picture my situation, imagine a funnel with its narrow tubular mouth that opens out to a wider receptacle. At the moment my position was in the middle of the tube.

As I swam toward the amphitheater I saw a long object that looked like a cigar with fins. Its grey-topped head nosed in my direction. Its white underside swung to and fro.

I glanced left and right, and realized that the tops of the underwater shelves were level with my shoulders. They were not a good place to swim onto for the predator could strike while my legs still dangled in the channel. Ahead of me the funnel broadened out giving me maneuver room. I swam forward even though the shark and I closed on each other.

The animal moved from thirty feet away to ten feet. Its right eye caught mine as it turned its body revealing its gaping jaws. Many times I had been told never to flee from the predator otherwise it would consider you prey and attack.

Although an insane fear gripped me, I willed my body to stand its ground. Would the creature smell my anxiety and strike? Its turning might be a sign that the shark intended to bite me, or was it? Maybe it just wanted to pass through? But the creature never eats head on, but sideways.

Downward the shark glided. Its great tail threshed the water. Its mouth aimed at my legs. "Shoot the gills," Jack had said.

With the turning movement the animal's breathing slits behind its eyes came into my view. Five feet away. I released my cocked spear. It struck into a soft area between the gills. I followed up my hit by sliding my fists to the penetration point then thrust my slender, spring-steel rod deeper into the breathing slits, and held on.

The reaction was fierce. It tried to dive. I forced it up. It shook its head from side to side. I held on tighter. Our battle brought us above the surface. I yelled, "Shark, shark."

Maybe realizing I called for help the critter pulled me under. My mouth tasted salty. I bubbled out water. I needed air. I kicked us to the surface. My lungs burned, I gulped. The creature's body threshed left and right. Under we went.

Then I saw the aluminum barb at the tip of my spear swinging. Less than two inches penetrated the creature. Soon it would work free of the spear.

Thrusting the rod in with one hand, I flung my other arm onto its side, grasping for its upright fin. Sand paper-like skin bruised my chest. My fingers clutched but failed to seize anything. My spear loosened with the shark's violent movements. Should I pull it out? Cock it and fire?

I felt the animal shudder, then shudder again. It pushed into me. My spear came loose. I rose to the surface. Cowboy went by me firing his weapon into the gills. I saw Ben and Jack on the opposite side. They had also speared the shark. No longer was it a fair fight.

The three men pulled the animal to the surface. Cowboy yelled, "Hit him again."

I did.

"What happened?" Jack said.

"The shark was going for my legs."

"Maybe your fish. They are dangling down between your feet."

I had caught a passel of nenue. They weighted my floating device toward the ocean floor.

"I don't know. I wasn't going to ask the shark if he wanted me or the fish."

"Shoot first, ask questions later," Jack said, a smile on his face.

The four of us wrestled the weakening animal onto the shore. It was heavy. We could not lift it, only drag it to the grass at the edge of the sand. Once we let go, the shark flopped a few times and then lay still. Its belly moved and out came a baby and then seven more all looking alike. For the second time in the summer I had killed a mother. Maybe that is why she moved slowly as it approached me? I don't know. Oh well, I could always brag, "I fought nine sharks with one spear."

Our Ni'ihau adventure ended with meeting Hawaiians from the village and having a great time. This was followed next morning by my finding a huge nest of nenue near the southern tip of the island. We filled our boat's ice chest and headed home.

Sunday evening my friend Sooky found me. "Bobby, how are your legs? I heard they were torn up."

"They're fine. What are you talking about?"

"Last night, the radio reported that Bobby was bitten by a shark while fishing at Ni'ihau. I knew you had gone there."

"It wasn't me," I said and then told him my story. It turned out that both sharks were of the same breed, black finned Threshers.

The days grew shorter. A glorious summer drew to a close. Decision time had arrived. I expressed my uncertainties to Aunt Maggie, a school teacher and a person filled with practical wisdom.

"I understand your feelings," she said. "You cannot hide from the realities of life by fleeing into the mountains of Kaua'i."

"I can go to Alaska and start over."

"And freeze to death. No, you must face up to responsibilities. Go to school. Be an attorney and come back and do something for Hawaii."

"But what chance would I have here? Everything is controlled by the Big Five."

"Japanese veterans are taking advantage of the GI Bill. They are going to college. It is an opportunity none of them had as long as their parents worked for the plantations. Once these boys are educated they will come back and make changes. Yutaka believes they will."

"What about Joseph?"

"Hamamoto and I are saving money for him to go to the university. You are fortunate your mother and father have enough right now to pay for Stanford. You must take advantage of it."

I left for California uncertain as to what to do. Resentment for having been left in Hawai'i for many years had built into an anger I barely suppressed. All during that time I had made decisions on my own. It is true that Kamehameha was a military school and you followed a routine, but there were many gaps when you made decisions for yourself. The events of a glorious summer and overcoming my fear of mano buoyed my belief that I could support myself.

My hostility became evident when I arrived in San Francisco, two days before the beginning of a week of orientation for incoming freshmen at Stanford. I expressed my thoughts that maybe I should go to Alaska and get a job.

"You must go to college and get an education," my father said. Your mother and I never had the opportunity. Go to Stanford, become a lawyer, return home and run the business."

Those were his final words. I chose not to argue thinking I could take my summer earnings, leave the house, and never come back. Late that night, I heard my mother scream. My father's doctor came. My dad died of a massive heart attack.

The week I would have spent in orientation at Stanford was spent in returning my father to Kaua'i. At his funeral his many friends came to bid him goodbye. He was remembered as "The Pioneer Showman of the Pacific".

When we were alone, my mother and sister said, "You must go to Stanford. Learn to be a lawyer and come back and run your father's enterprise."

With tears flowing from my eyes, shaken by my father's sudden death and our last argument, I said, "I will."

Epilogue

A black Southern Pacific locomotive, its engine blowing steam, squealed to a stop. I grabbed my suitcase, got off the train, heard its shrill whistle sound, and watched it pull away. The wheels of its eight passenger cars clicked and clacked in a jumble of noise that hurt my ears still smarting from my dive at Lehua Island.

Leland Stanford had made his fortune from the railroad. He had made his home on the fringe of the town of Palo Alto. When his only son died, the former governor of California willed much of his money and the land surrounding the small town to a school to be called Leland Stanford, Junior, University.

I trudged up Palm Drive, a mile long roadway bordered with royal palms. I crossed to the left of Memorial Church and Hoover tower to the men's gym. In front of me lay a broad expanse of green lawn and at its far end, Encina Hall, the dormitory for entering freshmen.

As I stepped onto the grass two round discs, like miniature flying saucers, wobbled toward me. They spun down, smacked, skipped, and came to rest near my feet. A voice from a fourth floor window called, "Stay right there. Don't move the discs. Watch them."

I waited.

Two young men came down the stairs of Encina and ran to me. The taller one looked vaguely familiar. Coming to where I stood, he said, "Tell us where each disc landed."

I pointed to the marks in the grass left by the missiles.

"I beat you," the taller man said. He turned. Looked at me for a moment then said, "Thanks. I'm Bob Mathias and this is Austin Petty, high school discus champ. We were having a competition."

Bob Mathias, Olympic Gold Medalist
In Decathalon

Oh, wow! I had met the star of the London Olympics. As we headed to the freshmen dormitory I listened to the two world class athletes exchange stories. We bid goodbye. I climbed to the third floor, found my assigned room, stored my gear, and walked to the men's toilet.

A robust, blonde, blue eyed, Germanic-looking young man was there. We introduced ourselves and exchanged information. "You're from Hawai'i? Do you know what these phrases mean, 'Come on I wanna lay ya' and 'Laka nuki.'"

"Oh yeah, that's ho'omalimali."

"What's that mean?"

"Bullshit."

We laughed and high-fived.

I returned to my room and met the army veteran with whom I would spend a year. "Call me Snuffy Smith," he said.

When I learned he would be taking courses in Russian language and history, I asked "Why?"

"The Soviet Union has got the atomic bomb. They have the biggest army in the world. Soon we will all be speaking Russian. I'm just getting prepared."

The next day as I hurried to sign up for courses my head buzzed with the knowledge that I would be taught by world class academics and Noble Prize winners. I would be meeting famous people and if I had good grades I might be admitted to a law school called, "The Harvard of the West." I knew I had made the right decision.

Great changes occurred in Hawai'i in the 1950s. The Japanese-American veterans took advantage of the G.I. Bill, went to college and law school. At the end of their schooling they joined the Democratic Party, and were instrumental in leading the 1954 peaceful revolution that seized control of the Territorial legislature from the Republicans. This political change meant that agricultural interests no longer ran the government.

Progressive taxation, land reform, and fairness to labor followed which affected the ability of the sugar plantations and pineapple canneries to be profitable. In 1959 Hawai'i became a state, giving the islands a more powerful role in Congress with two Senators and two House Representatives.

In 1962 John A. Burns was elected Governor and the Democratic Party took total control of state government. The demise of agri-business accelerated with the closure of pineapple canneries and sugar plantations, industries no longer able to compete in the world market place.

A bright light for the Hawaiian economy was the rise of tourism. In 1946 the hotel rooms numbered twelve hundred and the tourist arrivals less than forty thousand. With statehood, the movies made in Hawai'i, and the jet aircraft, tourism became the number one industry of the islands with multi-millions of visitors annually and billions of dollars spent. By the turn of the century tourism and defense spending were the key factors in sustaining the Hawaiian economy.

The aloha spirit which had declined during the war years revived with the influx of visitors and the movies made in the islands. Hawai'i born President Barrack Obama on the 50th Anniversary of Statehood said:

> "The Aloha Spirit of Hawai'i offers hope and opportunity for all Americans to learn from its diversity, how different cultures blend together into one population, made stronger by their shared sense of community."

After graduating from Stanford, I remained in California as an attorney and Superior Court Judge. Retired, I have returned home to live the stress-free life that Kaua'i gives you.

At Stanford University, California

About the Author

Bill Fernandez, half Native Hawaiian, was born and raised on the small island of Kaua'i in the Hawaiian Islands. After attending Kamehameha Schools he graduated from Stanford University and its law school. He practiced law in Sunnyvale, California, home of the future Silicon Valley, and served on the Sunnyvale City Council and as mayor.

Bill spent twenty years as judge of the Santa Clara County Courts, retired, and eventually returned to his island home. There, with his wife, Judith, he writes memoirs and novels, gives talks, served as president of the Kaua'i Historical Society, and enjoys the ocean breezes of his youth. They reside in the small cottage his mother bought with her pineapple earnings in the 1920s.

Official portrait of Judge William J.
Fernandez, Santa Clara County Courts, CA.

Book Review

A young teen at a Hawaiian military school near the end of World War II contemplates his future in Fernandez's (*Kaua'i Kids in Peace and War*, 2013, etc.) autobiographical series.

After retiring in California, Fernandez's father sent his 14-year-old, Hawaii-born son to military school in Honolulu. It was 1944, when the world was still at war. But even once the war was over, Hawaii remained at unrest: a labor union—on hold due to implementation of martial law—launched a workers' strike, while a tsunami hit Kauai and Hilo. Fernandez, who'd experienced racism in Hawaii, toured the mainland U.S. with his family and found a nation with unbridled prejudices and discrimination. His father wanted him to study to be a lawyer, leaving Fernandez, who feared Hawaiians might have no future in their homeland, to consider his options. The author's memoir is a riveting account of his experience in a world in disarray, both during and after the war. WWII is aptly displayed, particularly the pervasive fear of nuclear weapons as well as the worry of communists infiltrating America. But what makes the grandest impression is the more personal side of the narrative. Fernandez, for example, is Portuguese-Hawaiian, but his brown skin and surname lead some to mistake him for a Mexican, mistreating him accordingly. Similarly, his family witnessed a hotel clerk reject service for a Jewish couple after seeing the man's last name. In Tennessee, Fernandez had to stop and think about which of the segregated restrooms he could use, while the situation in Mexico proved equally appalling: just the lighter-skinned citizens, it seems, had jobs or money. Particularly regaling are Fernandez's descriptions of beaches surrounded by barbed-wire fences and fishing near the shore. Readers will be especially intrigued by events that brought Fernandez to his transformative decision to attend Stanford University.

Engrossing and identifiable.

— Kirkus Reviews